RACCOON GANGS, PIGEONS GONE BAD, & OTHER ANIMAL ADVENTURES

TRISH ANN KONIECZNY

TEN PEAKS PRESS™
EUGENE, OR

Bible translations quoted in this book can be found at end of the book.

Published in association with Books & Such Literary Management, 52 Mission Circle, Suite 122, PMB 170, Santa Rosa, CA 95409-5370, www.booksandsuch.com.

Cover design by Faceout Studio, Tim Green

Cover photo © Eric Isselee, Mrs_ya / Shutterstock

Interior designer Rockwell Davis

Photos © Trish Ann Konieczny

Photo editor Dawn Konieczny

Back cover photo © 2021 Mickey and Stacy Agee

Illustrations Lydia Charboneau © 2021 Trish Ann Konieczny

Names and minor details have been changed in the real-life stories shared in this book to protect the privacy of the individuals mentioned.

Information on zoonotic diseases and the risks associated with handling wildlife given in these pages is general in nature. This information is not professional medical counsel and should not be viewed as such. Neither the author nor the publisher assumes any liability for possible adverse consequences as a result of the information contained herein.

For bulk or special sales, please call 1-800-547-8979. Email: Customerservice@hhpbooks.com

TEN PEAKS PRESS is a trademark of the Hawkins Children's LLC. Harvest House Publishers, Inc., is the exclusive licensee of the trademark TEN PEAKS PRESS.

To the Lion of Judah,
in whose care every creature resides,
particularly here in the Lion's Den.

For all the animals of the forest are mine [says the Lord],
and I own the cattle on a thousand hills.
I know every bird on the mountains,
and all the animals of the field are mine.

PSALM 50:10-11

CONTENTS

1. A Cry in the Night. 7

2. Toddler Tornadoes. 15

3. Going Rounds with the Gang 23

4. The Ringtail Gang Parties On 31

5. Just the Beginning 43

6. The "Spark" of Life 47

7. Spark Finds a Family 53

8. Pigeon Gone Bad. 59

9. Flying in Under the Radar 67

10. Crazy Calls About Critters. 79

11. Cameo Shots and Comical Logs 87

12. Going Down a Rabbit Trail 99

13. The Difficult Days. 107

14. A Single Ringtail Tale. 117

15. Because He Cares, We Care 127

    Appendix: Favorite Animal Verses 133

    My Own Rescue Attempts:
    What Went Right, What Went Wrong 149

1

A CRY IN THE NIGHT

You called out in distress, and I rescued you.

PSALM 81:7 HCSB

"Something's crying outside, and it won't stop!" my husband, Michael, lamented late one evening. "I keep hearing it again and again. We ought to go out and find it."

So he did. A tiny raccoon kit with its eyes not yet open was letting us know it was not happy! Apparently, it had fallen quite some distance out of the monster cottonwood tree not far from our bedroom window, and its momma had not been down or around to rescue it yet. True to form, and because I'm supposedly the animal nut, Michael hauled this kit into the house and said to me, "What are *you* going to do with it?"

All curled up in the bottom of a five-gallon bucket, the little raccoon was emitting a noise that was echoing alarmingly around our heads. *Anything to stop that screeching*, I thought to myself. "Let's call a wildlife rehabilitator to find out what *we* should do with it," I said aloud.

We found a number online for someone who rescued wildlife in our county and gave her a call.

"Reunite it with its mother; that's the best thing for it," she said. "And here's how…"

She gave us detailed instructions that involved putting the kit outside in a loosely covered container under the tree so its mother could retrieve it during the night. She said trying to reunite babies with mothers that way often worked well, and she was quite sure this small ringtail would be safely back in its raccoon family fold by morning.

We followed her instructions to the letter and went to bed. Figuring we'd done the best we could, I didn't think much more about it and drifted off to sleep. But Michael is a lighter sleeper than I am. Even the vibrating of our phones—the vibrating, mind you, not the ringing—can wake him out of a sound sleep. And the wild things around our neck of the woods make a lot of nighttime noise. An owl is always hooting, coyotes are howling, or some late-night critter is squeaking outside the window. So my husband is awakened a lot.

This particular night, however, Michael found one sound even more distracting than all the rest. About 5:30 in the morning, bleary-eyed, he nudged me. "I didn't sleep much at all. That raccoon baby is *still* crying! It's been crying *all* night! I'm going out to take a look."

That's when he discovered that it was raining raccoons. Or technically, it was raining raccoon kits. Down in the brush beneath the old cottonwood, he kept finding tiny raccoons, one after the other, each squirming around desperately in search of its mother. After several minutes of wading through the underbrush, he had come upon four of them.

Again he brought the tiny raccoons into the house, all curled up in the bottom of the bucket, and asked me, true to form, "What are *you* going to do with all these babies now?"

If you've never heard a baby raccoon screeching, you've missed out on one of life's most pitiable experiences, not to mention one of life's loudest distractions. (Count your blessings.) *One baby screeching last night was pitiful enough, but four is unbearable!* I thought to myself. "We'll have to call the wildlife rehabilitator back to see what to do next," I said aloud.

I went into another room, hoping to be able to hear myself think, and got on the phone. "I'm calling to give you a report on the raccoon kit from last night. We did exactly as you said and put it out in a loosely covered container so its mother could retrieve it during the night. She never came for it, and now three more babies have rained down from the tree. There are four in all, and one seems quite weak."

"That's not good!" she said. "They're probably dehydrated. If Momma had been there during the night, they'd have full bellies and be content. They wouldn't have been crawling around last night and falling out of the den. They were trying to find her, but apparently she has disappeared. You'd better bring them in to me."

So these four loud little fuzzy heads and I got into the car and traveled 45 minutes to the rehabber's house. Thankfully, the kits were mostly quiet on the way, either lulled to sleep or terrified by the car's noise and motion. It had been a long night for us all, and I was looking forward to getting the poor little things into the hands of an expert and traveling back to my own nest in peace.

Do or Die

"Oh my, yes, they're very dehydrated," this rehabilitation expert said, weighing and examining the tiny ring-tailed orphans on our arrival. "I don't know where their momma is, but these little ones have not been fed in quite a while. Why don't you help me get some electrolytes into them?"

"Great! I'd love to!" I didn't get to handle wildlife babies every day, and these baby raccoons were hugely appealing—at least when they weren't screeching.

The rehabber mixed up electrolyte bottles and showed me what to do. We each took a couple of babies and got some rehydrating liquid into their stomachs. In the process, I quizzed her about the work she did with wildlife. I saw a pail labeled "raccoon formula" sitting nearby and asked her the obvious question: "Where on earth do you get raccoon formula?"

"Oh, a lot of rehabilitators use wildlife milk formulas like this one from companies that specialize in making them. This formula is especially good. It's a milk replacer you can use from day one with tiny raccoons, and they do really well on it. I can buy good species-specific formulas for all the babies we get in. The protein and fat content of the mother's milk is different for every animal, and orphan wildlife babies do much better if they're given exactly the right formula for their species. You can try raising them on kitten milk replacer or puppy milk replacer, but those can end up causing a host of problems in the long run."

Who knew such a thing as raccoon formula and squirrel formula and fox formula and opossum formula existed? I certainly didn't—yet she had it all.

"This formula isn't cheap!" she went on. "Raccoon milk powder is 12 dollars a pound, and a pound doesn't last long at all with a litter of four. But it's worth it."

"Now that these four babies have something filling their tiny little tummies, what happens next with them?" I asked.

"Let me show you something," the rehabber said. She led me into another room that contained five good-sized wire dog crates. Each crate contained a single raccoon kit roving around inside it. Each kit was climbing up the side of its crate and grabbing things or rolling around and play-biting stuffed animals. Between the five of them in those individual crates, they were raising a ruckus that filled the whole room. They were bigger and more mobile than the babies I had brought in, but were still quite small.

"Why are they all separated?" I asked.

"Raccoons can carry distemper, among other things. It's highly contagious and deadly to them. They each have to be quarantined for two weeks if they come in as single babies. If they stay healthy during that time, they can then be put in together. It's really good for them to live with their own kind, but people mostly bring me rescued singles that have to go through quarantine first. This is all the room I have available for raccoons, and you can see that every crate is occupied. Right now, I'm full!"

"Okay, what about other rehabbers in the area?" I asked.

"There is one," she said, "but I know she's full too. And due to the diseases they carry, raccoons must be released within whatever Michigan county they're born in. So I'm sorry, but you'll have to take these four you found home with you. I can't keep them here. Either you'll have to try raising them yourself, or you'll have to take them to your vet and have them euthanized."

When it rains raccoons, it pours.

She gave me a minute or two to digest that unexpected and shocking news, and then she asked, "What do you want to do?"

I may be the animal nut, but I had Michael's reaction in mind when I tentatively and with much trepidation answered, "Okay, then, how do I keep them alive at home?"

"I'll give you the electrolytes and formula and all the help you need anytime you want to call me," she said. (Now that I think back on it, she said those words almost gleefully.) "And I can fill out paperwork for the state agency in charge of wildlife so you can do this legally. You can become registered as a sub-permittee—a bottle-feeder who helps me raise orphans under my wildlife rehabilitator license. Once they're weaned, you'll bring them back to me here for release, or we'll decide where else to release them."

And so it began...and it hasn't ended yet. But she wasn't quite done with me: "If you're going to give this a try, the first thing we'd better do is worm them. You have to worm them every two weeks and *never, never* miss doing it!" she stressed. "They carry raccoon roundworm, which isn't dangerous to them, but it's dangerous to *you*. People think raccoons carry rabies, but there hasn't been a rabid raccoon in Michigan for more than 20 years. It's the roundworms you have to worry about. They can migrate into the human brain."

Great, I thought, *now I feel like worming myself!* (Actually, I do worm myself now that I work with wildlife regularly, but I'll spare you that story right at the start.) Still, I took the four tiny kits home anyway, roundworms and all, along with a hefty supply of worming medicine and everything else necessary for a human to become their mother hen.

I walked through the door back home 45 minutes later, and in an odd reversal I handed my husband the bucketful of raccoons and said, "What are *we* going to do with these now?"

"Why on earth do you still have them?" he asked.

I told him the whole story about the rehabber's facility being full of raccoons and the other rehabber being full of raccoons and everyone in our whole county who worked with wildlife (all of three people) being full of raccoons. Then I told him our choices: It was do or die.

"We should have them euthanized," he said decisively.

Then he added, "How often do they need to be fed? What kind of cage will they need? How will we tell them apart? Do you have to get up at night to feed them?" (Notice the *you*.)

He finished with, "Quick, you'd better mix up some bottles! I think they're hungry." (Notice the *you* again.)

Baby ringtail getting used to the bottle

The Calm Before the Storm

Truly, I didn't object at all to the feeding and cleaning and care suddenly thrust upon my schedule by the addition of four furry babies to our household. I have always been an animal fan, although I might not go so far as to call myself a fanatic. (Others might, like my husband.) As usual with any animals, I found these four tiny creatures fascinating and wildly (pun intended) appealing.

Did you know, for instance, that tiny raccoons purr when their mother comes back to the nest and nuzzles or licks them as they start to nurse? I had no idea they purred, or perhaps more accurately, churred, like that! As soon as I would begin to stroke a kit at feeding time, out of its throat would come this excited little sound that expressed how very happy it was to find "Momma" and how thrilled it was to start eating. Its whole body would vibrate with the effort. It didn't take me long to get caught up in the excitement of mothering this foursome and start churring back.

But then I frequently find furry animals distracting, along with the birds of the air, the creatures of the sea, and anything with an exoskeleton or eight legs. Sometimes I have to work to stay focused on the things that really matter—or should really matter to me as a Christian and formerly a pastor's wife—for example, human beings with human needs of spirit, soul, and body.

In my defense, I think Jesus found all creatures great and small captivating too. When He spent 40 days in the desert, Scripture tells us "he was with the wild animals" (Mark 1:13 NIV). Animals are everywhere, yet they get a special mention for being around Jesus at that trying time in His life. They might not have been sitting in His lap—or they might have been. We don't know. Yet I'm guessing that their nearness provided Him with some comfort and companionship, and I understand that. I want to be with the wild animals, too, for the same reasons. It certainly felt companionable to hold the fuzzy raccoon kits in my arms and feed them!

I often think that whenever animals were near Jesus, the feeling of companionship must have gone both ways. I believe the animals knew when they were in the presence of their Creator. Think about the scene on Palm Sunday: Jesus climbs on the back of a colt that has never been ridden before and then rides it through the middle of a cheering, boisterous crowd of people who are shouting "Hosanna in the highest!" at the top of their lungs (see Mark 11:1-10). It is highly unlikely that any of us could have stayed on that colt without the scene turning into quite a rodeo. To stay so calm and obliging, that colt must have known something about the One who was on his back and must have trusted Him completely. Matthew 21 tells us that Jesus made sure the colt's mother was brought along, undoubtedly as a means of comforting the colt in such unusual surroundings. I am convinced that God greatly cares about and enjoys all His creatures, many of which have played such interesting parts in biblical history right from the start.

Likewise, I began enjoying the job of caring for these four orphan raccoons. At the early stage, all they did was eat (a lot) and go to the bathroom (a lot) and sleep (a lot)…and sleep (a lot)…and sleep (a lot). As long as their stomachs were full, they were content to stay put in a soft blanket nest, quiet and relaxed. They were still too young to do anything else, and I was too inexperienced to know what was coming. I didn't quite realize that this peaceful stage wouldn't last long. As we were about to find out, what started out as a little bit of a raccoon rainstorm would soon turn into some wild, wild weather! We were about to have four very active, furry tornadoes on our hands.

2

TODDLER TORNADOES

Suddenly, a powerful wind swept in from the wilderness.

JOB 1:19

M y rescuer husband and I spent a couple of blissful weeks as new raccoon parents. The fun part was that raccoon orphans need a ton of tender, loving care, which helps bolster their will to live. Area rehabbers told us it was fine to give them all the TLC we wanted to at first, at least while they were still babies.

Everything got off to what seemed like a great start. It didn't even cost us much. The rehabilitator had given me plenty of that specialized raccoon formula worth its weight in gold, plenty of electrolyte mix for their first week, plenty of wormer, and plenty of instructions to get us started.

I soon became used to mixing bottles, which I'd never had to do as a human mom since I had nursed my own kids. Soon I got on a (barely) manageable schedule of feeding the babies every few hours. I even grew to like the smell of raccoon milk powder, and I still do. You probably would, too, if you smelled it. The odor is sweet, milky, and hearty at the same time. Getting the milk into the front end of the babies was quite satisfying.

The not-so-fun part was cleaning the babies up at the other end afterward, the way their wild momma would have. Many animal mothers stimulate their babies at the back end to help them urinate and defecate. That way, the moms can make sure all the waste is removed

15

from the nest (one way or the other), so their babies stay clean and the odor doesn't attract predators.

You don't want to know the messy details of how I tried to duplicate that process as a human wildlife mom. All you need to picture in your mind is that whatever liquid and/or solid poo came out, it came

This juvenile Gangster still wants a bottle

out quickly. Very quickly. Everywhere. Soon my goal was to become proficient at positioning each kit over a trash can lined with paper towels during the cleanup process. My hope was that my aim would be better than the kit's, but I never had been very good at hitting a target.

Practice makes perfect, however, and with multiple mouths to feed and multiple nether ends to clean up, I had no shortage of opportunities to aim for my goal. Besides, it simply had to be done. Many wild babies can't go to the bathroom on their own for days or even weeks, so if they are orphaned and their human rescuers feed them but don't take care of business at the other end, the bladder pressure and toxic effects build up so much inside the babies that they cannot survive. I would not have known that without some training from a rehabber.

What made me think that cleaning cages later on would be easier than cleaning back ends—I don't know, but suffice it to say that cleaning up poo in any form at any stage by any method is less than fun. That much I can now tell you from lots and lots of experience.

The Trouble with Toddlers

As the babies grew and became much more vocal (screechy) and much more mobile (16 grabby paws a minute), mothering four raccoon kits sometimes rivaled what I imagine it would be like to have four human toddlers around at once. I'm not sure how else to describe it. We have three children of our own, but they came one toddler at a time. Now that they are grown, married, and having children of their own, I've experienced what it is like to have half a dozen grandchildren around who all want Grandma's attention at once, and I love the welcome chaos. But even that doesn't rival the chaos of taking care of four toddler-aged raccoons. One minute they were tiny specks of fur sleeping softly and soundly in a warm nest all day; the next minute they were toddler tornadoes taking life by storm, and we were blindsided.

Yet parents still love their toddlers who are making trouble, and some even love toddler quadruplets. If only they weren't so cute (human or raccoon). I couldn't help feeling attached to these little bundles, especially when they were sweetly sleeping together in a ball of fluff, rare though it became for all four to be asleep at once. We even gave them names, which can be wise or unwise as a rehabber, depending on how well you can control your level of attachment. These four became Skeeter (short for "mosquito" as he was always grabbing something, including me, with his mouth), Sharky (because he went beyond grabbing, straight to nipping), Golden Boy (because he was lighter in color than the rest, almost a blonde raccoon), and Ducky (I don't remember why, but what an odd name, I now think).

If their names aren't clue enough, did I mention that all four of them were males? What are the odds? In a way, that worked in my favor. Boy raccoons go wild and usually leave for good, so it's not as if these would be underfoot forever. Girls go wild, but sometimes will return in subsequent spring seasons to show off their babies. That sounded somewhat appealing, but I wouldn't be having that pleasure out of this litter.

Each one of these guys was all boy! The weak among them got stronger, the small got bigger, and they grew and grew. After their eyes opened and their coordination kicked in, their grabbing and climbing and running began in earnest. If you've never tried to open a cage door and do some necessary task while four juvenile raccoons make a beeline for the exit all at once, you've never really faced an animal challenge and prevailed. Come to think of it, I rarely prevailed myself. But I expended a lot of effort trying.

Nothing Straightforward About It

Let me digress and make a quick disclaimer before I tell any more of this tale. If you are a professional animal person yourself, maybe a biologist or state game officer or another rehabber, keep in mind as I describe this first time around that I was learning about working with wildlife. I was *in training*. I didn't do everything right, and I did a lot of things wrong that I wouldn't do again. I even got a fair amount of conflicting advice from rehabbing experts. I refined the process in the following seasons, dropped a lot of dumb things I had done at the start, and added a lot of important things I initially overlooked.

But this first time around I didn't do everything wrong, either, as evidenced by the woods camera out back (an outdoor camera that captures videos or stills of wildlife), which is still catching photos of what I believe are some of the raccoons from this first bunch in all their wildness, even as I write these pages a couple of years later. So be merciful as you read about my first attempts at raising orphan raccoon kits. It's not like rehabbing raccoons is all that easy or straightforward in the best of circumstances.

In fact, almost all the experts agree on one thing: Raccoons are far and away the hardest mammals to rehabilitate successfully—not so much in keeping them alive and healthy, but in keeping yourself sane and healthy in the process. The statistics certainly back that up. In my home state of Michigan, and no doubt in countless others, many licensed wildlife rehabilitators specialize in two things—taking in a certain favorite species, and *not* taking in raccoons.

If you look at online lists of rehabbers county by county, entry after entry will include the qualifier "*No raccoons.*" That has less to do with raccoons being an RVS—rabies vector species—and more to do with their being what I call a DVS—delinquency vector species. As the saying among rehabbers goes, "You can do raccoons, or you can do everything else, but you can't do both!" So I figure it must be worth something that I survived rehabbing a litter of four male raccoon kits all the way to release on my first attempt.

Despite the challenges the first time presented, rehabbing had its bonus features. For hours and hours, I could have watched this first litter wrestle with each other, squeal, shimmy up anything with their busy paws, and play with water of any sort (bowls, pans, drips, drops, anything the least bit wet). For hours and hours, I often did watch them. They were far more entertaining than television.

The Ringtail Gang

These four guys cooked up all sorts of mischief—raccoons aren't called ring-tailed rascals for nothing. I couldn't imagine it in my wildest dreams, but some people keep a raccoon for a pet. What would be left of a house? Besides being unpredictable (if not dangerous) when they mature, raccoons leave nothing untouched. You've heard the saying "What's mine is mine, and what's yours is mine"? I'm pretty sure a raccoon said it first. These guys were not all for one but each one for himself.

The kits always made a beeline for anything new they set their shiny little eyes on. They could never resist grabbing it, exploring it, tasting it, or chewing it up. And it seemed as if they had the longest reach of any animal on the planet. No matter how far away from their cage I set an item, one of them would manage to snag it, pull it between the bars, and start a full-scale riot over it. Especially if it was a set of keys— either real ones or toys. You've seen those little colored plastic key sets made for human babies? Baby raccoons *cannot* get enough of those, so it's a good thing I rarely find a garage sale without a used plastic key set going cheap or free because the keys usually have teeth marks in them. Raccoon kits don't care who has chewed what before them.

Soon I was calling these sweet babies—which were fast turning into juvenile delinquents—the Ringtail Gang for short. I meant it in a Mafia sort of way. It's how they operated. They were quickly learning how to employ every underhanded scheme the term *gangster* implies to get what they wanted or to do what they wanted. I've gained so much insight into the criminal mind from rehabbing raccoons!

Like any respectable mobsters, they certainly were extortionists. If they had something I wanted, or if they had planted themselves somewhere I didn't want them to be, I knew I would have to ante up with some pretty high-stakes payoffs to get any cooperation from them. Usually that involved something sweet or something shiny, or both.

Sometimes to preserve my sanity, I would shut them into our enclosed side porch while I cleaned their cage, just so I didn't have to wrestle with them. All four of them always wanted to be involved in every little cleaning task, dirtying everything all over again before I ever got anything clean. Or they all wanted *out* the cage door when I wanted them to stay *in*. To sidestep the daily rumble, I would float a few handfuls of grapes, one of their first and favorite solid foods, in a big pan of water out on the porch. Then I would pop the gang out there to practice their fishing skills while I tidied up their digs. That made for good multitasking, as they learned a skill they would need in the wild while I accomplished my very necessary cleaning task.

Once the gang's cage was livable again (by human standards), I would pop out to the porch too, refill the pan with grapes, and watch the show. You know how raccoons love water, and they certainly love tasty grapes, so it was a hoot to see their excitement over this activity. It caused quite a wet and crazy uproar, which was fine with me (although I then had to clean the porch).

The glitch in the plan came whenever it was time to catch them and put them back inside their clean cage. You would not believe how many hiding places a relatively small and fairly empty side porch contains in the minds of four raccoons looking to make a fast getaway. One would squeeze under the cedar chest I could barely get one finger under myself. Another would squeeze behind it, where I thought there wasn't so much as the smallest sliver of room. A third would disappear down the toe of a muck boot, making it hard at that odd angle to get a handle on anything but teeth. A fourth would somehow scamper into a cabinet I thought was firmly latched and then burrow behind anything to stay out of sight and out of reach (and usually knocking everything over in the process). Besides honing their fishing skills on the porch, the gang got a lot of practice at hiding out in unreachable places. That was also a skill that would stand them in good stead once they were released into the wild, but I wasn't all that fond of them practicing it on me!

All too soon—and at the same time not nearly soon enough—the Ringtail Gang grew big enough that it became a challenge to keep them content in a cage when they weren't out for exercise, or even to keep them happy playing on our enticing little porch. The time was coming to let our little group of gangsters take over some new territory.

3

GOING ROUNDS WITH THE GANG

Do you not know that in a race all the runners run, but only
one gets the prize? Run in such a way as to get the prize.

1 Corinthians 9:24 niv

As Skeeter, Sharky, Golden Boy, and Ducky were weaned off bottles and onto solid foods, they needed more room to run and more exposure to life's wild side. I set up a much larger play cage for them back in the woods, just beyond the border of our yard. It was far enough away from the house to remove the gang from most human noise and activity, yet close enough for me to hear them screech if any trouble arose. I also figured it was far enough away to remove them from getting into too much trouble around the house and yard once they started spending time outside the cage rather than in it (which would prove to be wishful thinking on my part).

Each morning I would bottle-feed the Ringtail Gang, stick them into pet carriers, and haul them out to the play cage for the day. At first they were a little taken aback, but soon they were peering out from the safety of their beloved hammock, which hung high up in the cage. With great interest, they began to take in all the sights and sounds of the wild world where they would eventually be released.

Midmorning and midafternoon I took pans of formula-soaked food out to the release cage. The milky raccoon formula on top of the edible offerings was meant to entice them into feeding themselves more, so I could take a break from the weeks of constant bottle-feeding and feed them by hand a lot less. Thankfully, it didn't take long for the gang to begin to crave it all, from puppy chow to Cheerios to PB and Js. They started eating almost everything with great gusto, with the notable exception of vegetables. Anyone who thinks raccoons are raiding a vegetable garden just might be mistaken. The boys turned up their noses at green beans, lettuce, and tomatoes. From their expressions when I tried to offer them a carrot, you'd think I was the very scum of the earth.

Fruit was a different story. These guys were fanatically fruity! Fruit was all they needed in any form to make them totally, blissfully, completely happy. Applesauce, frozen berries, bananas, bananas, bananas. I had never purchased so many bananas in all my life. The store people got to know me because I was constantly haunting the produce aisles in my never-ending search for "red-tape" bananas. Every now and again a store would fill a grocery cart almost full of the deeply discounted bananas, and I would come in and buy the entire thing. The workers thought I had either lost my mind or had a serious addiction to banana bread. The latter wasn't so much the case, but the former was arguably true by then.

Pinky and the Brain Revisited

Once the four gang members were highly mobile and had adjusted to being in the outside play cage in the woods, one rehab mentor told me to start letting them out for some wilderness survival training. That meant I was supposed to walk through the woods at a slow pace, and the kits were supposed to follow—or so the theory went.

At first I didn't believe it would ever happen that way once I opened the cage door. I didn't think it would be humanly possible to keep track of these four juveniles let loose upon the world. Yet I knew that if they ever were going to be released into the wild, I needed to take this next step with them. I needed to start taking them for walks on the wild side, as a raccoon mother would, and deal with whatever fallout resulted.

Raccoon kits follow their mommas through the woods all over the place, up and down trees, in and out of creeks, through the tall grass— all without getting lost. To my astonishment, these guys did the same with me. The theory that they would follow me as closely as they would have followed their own mother actually proved true! I tested it time and time again. No matter how tall a tree the four of them climbed without me, if I moved off in another direction, those four furballs high-tailed it down the tree to stick with me. That development was a huge relief when they were small, vulnerable to predators, and out on the loose for the first few times.

Of all the stages of rehabbing raccoons, leading them on woods walks became my very favorite. I spent hours leading these little softball-sized pipsqueaks around in the woods out back, often with Michael in tow just for fun. They had a glorious time exploring everything they could get their paws on, going up and down trees (and sometimes falling in this practice stage), and tasting anything and everything that caught their beady little eyes and looked the least bit enticing.

The walks also became the Ringtail Gang's favorite thing to do, of course. As soon as I opened their cage, they'd stream out and fall in line behind me, a fearsome foursome bent on taking over the world. They reminded me of a cartoon my kids used to watch, *Pinky and the Brain*. The show was so funny I couldn't help but watch it with the kids. The theme song talks about how one mouse is genius and the other insane. The genius mouse plots and plans all night every night, so that at dawn the two of them can take over the world. If that doesn't describe the Ringtail Gang's approach to life, I don't know what does. It was a riot to watch them growing up and gaining confidence, as if they knew that there wasn't much, at least in our part of the world, that would take on a male raccoon and win. The world was becoming their oyster.

The gang and I would traipse through the forest day after day on meandering explorations with me as their "teacher"—a loose term in this case for a substitute mother they could follow around who would also feed them at day's end. I figured that on these walks I could, at the least, give them some early exposure to the new wild world they would occupy. At the most, wonder of wonders, they might accidentally discover for themselves something to eat along the way. That made the daily excursions worth the time and effort—and heat and bugs and spider webs and sweat (none of which bothered them; only me).

Watching Skeeter and the gang snake through the tall grass behind me or move at a good clip down the trail so they wouldn't lose sight of

"Mom" was hilarious. It was heady stuff that tempted me to feel as if I really had this mothering raccoons thing down. Overall, everything felt nicely under control in my new rehabbing adventure.

Battle of Wits in the Wilderness

Alas, feelings can lie. Things were indeed under control, but the question was, Whose control? The answer would depend on who would win the battle of wits that began on these wilderness walks. I had never expected at the start to wind up going round after round with raccoons, but I was only just beginning to comprehend the kind of stamina and strategy that matching wits with the gang would require. Because there came a day when these gangsters were old enough and large enough to look after themselves, theoretically. They were not so vulnerable to predators anymore, and my mentor said I should lead them out into the woods in the morning and start leaving them there on "day release." The idea was that they would run around in our back-woods all day, exploring on their own and having whatever kind of raccoon fun they could drum up between the four of them.

The problem was, the thing that most appealed to Skeeter and the gang was to keep tagging along with me. I would lead them out to some enticing spot in the woods, and from the instant I tried to sneak away, they *still* followed me relentlessly. They simply did not want to sign up for the plan of staying wild and free all day without Mom. I had hoped to have my days free (read raccoon-free) and simply show up in the woods again in the early evenings to locate the boys and bring them back to the relative safety of their cage, away from any predators foolish enough to try to take on nearly full-grown raccoons. It seemed like a workable plan to one of the five of us, but I would have to go some rounds to persuade the other four. Our battle of wits went something like this:

Round 1—Lead the Ringtail Gang out back to the weather creek full of merrily trickling water, strew some PB and J sandwiches around as a snack, and *run like fire* for home, mistakenly optimistic that the boys would have so much fun eating their picnic fare and playing in the water that they would forget all about following me. Not so. By the time I approached the house and slowed down, they were all on my tail.

Round 2—Lead the Ringtail Gang to the tallest cottonwood tree way out back with the most branches to climb, let them get way up high to scamper back and forth overhead, and *run like fire* for home. I didn't factor in that from their perch high up in the leafy canopy, they could easily scope out the lay of the land and see which way I was heading. I would approach the house and slow down to catch my breath raggedly, glancing back just in case...yep, all on my tail.

Round 3—Lead the Ringtail Gang to the swampy area out back, scatter enough Honey Nut Cheerios and bananas to feed an army of four for an hour, back myself out of sight around the nearest, thickest tree trunk, and *run like fire* for home. My hope was that beetles, frogs, bugs, and bogs would be more mesmerizing to them than I was. But before I could even get near the house and slow down to catch my breath, a couple of them would pass me by. By this time, they really needed to stay out in the woods and learn how to be *wild*. Instead, they just wanted to sit under the porch and wait for me to come out of the house and take them for a walk. If I didn't come out soon enough to suit them, one or the other of the four would climb up the porch rail and jiggle the doorknob to see if he could come in and find me. That made it hard to get in and out of the house, for one thing. And it made the mailman and the FedEx guy think we were kind of strange, for another.

Round 4—This putting some distance between the Ringtail Gang and me so they could go wild was not going smoothly. I put in a call to one of my favorite rehab mentors. (I was consulting more than one by then because raising my first raccoon kits was making me feel less in control every day, and I needed all the advice I could get.) Our resulting conversation was less than helpful:

Me: Hello...about those four raccoons you've been helping me with. I can't get away from them!

Mentor: That's to be expected. You know they stay with Momma and each other all through the first winter? These little ones don't have Momma; they have *you*.

Me (wondering why I could hear her laughing): But I can't stay in the woods all day with them, and they won't stay in the woods by themselves and let me go back to the house. I mean, it's good for my health, I suppose, since I'm losing a ton of weight running away from raccoons on these blistering hot summer days, but I'm exhausted. What should I do?

Mentor: Keep running! This is why rehabbing raccoons through to release takes so much longer and can be so much more challenging than rehabbing almost any other animal. But they *will* eventually detach from you a little and stay out there with each other. Meanwhile, *run!*

Me (wondering why I could still hear her laughing): But they're so fast that they catch me—and a lot of times they beat me back to the house and wait for me. No matter where I go, there they are!

Mentor: My advice is to make yourself some new escape trails. Never go the same way twice; take a different way back to the house every time. And if they keep following you, just go into the house, shut the windows and doors, and *ignore* them. Eventually, they'll decide that playing in the woods all day is a lot more fun than waiting around outside your door for you.

My mentors were brilliant. Their suggestions were brilliant. I tried them all, in all their brilliance. Still, the doorknob rattled on rather frequent occasion. Without even looking outside, I knew who—or rather what (four whats)—would be there.

Mom, come out!

I tried to make the best of it. How many times in a lifetime, after all, does a person get to have a gang of raccoons knocking on the door? And to be fair, I had to remember that according to one mentor, juvenile raccoons typically remain with their mother through their first winter. I was asking these guys to let go of "Mom" early, so I'd just have to be patient in the process. Surely, I thought, they would grow to a point where the ring-tailed ladies would seem more enticing to them than I did. That was my theory, and I dearly hoped it would soon prove true. That day, however, was not yet...

4

THE RINGTAIL GANG PARTIES ON

*Above all, keep loving one another earnestly, since
love covers a multitude of sins. Show hospitality
to one another without grumbling.*

1 PETER 4:8-9 ESV

I'm sure that passage above was not intended to refer to animals, but it was a good one for Michael to keep in mind as our growing Ringtail Gang put our patience to the test. He wasn't above a little grumbling, however, and the raccoons weren't above committing a multitude of sins.

I myself was just about to expire from going round after round with them in the woods. I suppose the challenge of mothering raccoons *was* actually good for my health, as I really had developed new stamina and lost weight by running away from them on those hot summer days. But I was exhausted. *Surely there must be easier ways to get healthy and lose weight,* I thought, *like train for a marathon, go on a liquids-only diet— anything but try to outwit this gang of very determined raccoons!*

I spent a few more weeks playing chase during the day, but by then the Ringtail Gang had grown big enough to be out and about at night too. I left their familiar cage open wide all night so they could come and go, and they genuinely seemed to like the arrangement—so long as come bedtime, they could retreat into our wide-open garage to snooze rather than into their wide-open cage or the wide-open woods where they belonged.

Our garage was actually an ancient hewn-beam structure, the kind with gigantic planed logs that fit together without nails. It was built to house livestock in the 1800s, not cars in the twenty-first century. Once the ancient barn doors had rotted and fallen off, a former property owner installed a garage door that sort of fit and sort of didn't. By the time we bought the place as a vacant old farmhouse, that garage door was in serious disrepair and was far more trouble than it was worth to open and close. We took it off entirely, blissfully unaware of what that decision would mean in regard to this future Ringtail Gang. In retrospect, it's clear that tight-fitting garage doors are a marvelous invention, as everyone who has found a mouse nest in a car's air filter knows.

But we didn't have any such garage door, so the rafters of our ancient barn/garage became the gangsters' nighttime headquarters, rest area (like pull over and go to the bathroom), and breakfast deli all rolled into one. My reminders to them that their familiar woods cage and homey hammock were available nearby fell on deaf, though attractively fuzzy, ears.

Don't Rock the Boat!

We had stored important things in the garage rafters—for example, our four lime-green Otter kayaks that we so enjoyed, turned upside down. They weren't Otter kayaks anymore, however. They were raccoon kayaks now. Apparently, our motherless waifs voted unanimously that the noses of the kayaks were the perfect place in which to take up their first non-cage residence. This in spite of my husband having cobbled together a nice little wooden nesting box that he installed, of all places, on top of the kayaks.

But the Ringtail Gang didn't want to live *on top* of the boats; they wanted to live *inside* them. And to make the boats more comfy, they helped themselves to the Styrofoam float panels each contained, apparently voting them the ideal nesting material. Soon Styrofoam pieces were floating down from above like snow.

Was I happy that it didn't look as if we'd be going paddling anytime soon—like not till next year? Not at all. Our family had been enjoying kayaking for some time. Was Michael happy about it? He was ecstatic.

For all my husband's willingness to go along on kayak outings, he hated getting wet. He had bought himself one of those kayak "skirts" that you fasten around you once you're in the boat, so that not one single, solitary drop of water could breach your defenses and get you wet. And he never tipped over for fun (or otherwise) like the rest of us; he preferred to stay bone-dry even on the hottest of days. All things considered, the use (or misuse in this case) of the green Otter kayaks was not a big loss to him, which worked in the Ringtail Gang's favor big-time.

A Brand-New Rest Area

It became a never-ending raccoon party up in those garage rafters. I'd walk outside in the mornings and find the raccoons all hung over— I mean literally hanging over—the middle rafter. They'd all be looking toward the house and hoping I'd come out soon and hand each of them a banana to start their day. Or more appropriately, to end their night. They'd wolf down whatever I had to offer them, and then they'd waddle off into the noses of the kayaks for a full day's sleep. Sometimes they'd even oversleep from one day into the next as fall began to set in and the evenings grew progressively cooler. Wildlife rehabilitators keep daily animal care logs, and in one log entry I wrote:

> No Ringtail Gang picture today because it has been two long days since there has been any sign of activity from the den, and—this is stupid—I *miss* the little blighters! I've been waiting *weeks* for them to go to sleep and leave me in peace, and now I have this intense longing to lay eyes on them and feed them a banana. What's *wrong* with me that I miss them when they're sleeping?

But when the raccoons were up, they were up and hard at it. Then how I wished they'd go back to sleep! They even installed a "rest area" on the side of the garage opposite where they slept. For that particular home improvement, they had completely failed to get the necessary permits with their local "zoning board."

As the property's official owners, I assure you we were less than pleased to find out about this development. The extra boards we had stored up in the garage seemed to make a perfect litter pan holder, and oh, how the guys made use of the winter sled we had left sitting on those boards. They decided it was the ideal litter pan. The sled even matched the lime green of the kayaks, so the raccoons' loft decor was color coordinated. That seemed fitting because even though raccoons are poorly able to distinguish color, their eyes are well-adapted to see green light. I can't prove it scientifically, but maybe that had something to do with their fondness for the kayaks and sled.

I don't know how many times I emptied that green sled and cleaned out their rest area, hoping to discourage them from using that potty spot. Alas, raccoons are not easily discouraged. From the time they learn to walk, they pick a potty spot and rarely deviate from it. Everybody eliminates in the chosen spot every day. Even in the wild, raccoons are quite uniform about their rest area visits. This habit can be a nice feature when orphan raccoons are still caged and you can install a litter pan with sand or paper towels so all your cleanup is at least confined to a single spot. It's not so nice when the one spot they choose outside happens to be an area of value to local human residents, as anyone knows whose garage or attic has been taken over by raccoons.

If cleaning out the sled were all there was to it, it still would have been an unhappy chore. But it would have been less of a misery if I had not also felt as though I needed a hazmat suit to safely dispose of the raccoon waste. I didn't have a hazmat suit, but there were several times that I wished I were fully garbed in one. Remember those raccoon roundworms I mentioned at the start, when the rehabber showed me how to deworm the boys? Did I mention that they can migrate into the human brain?

A little caution is a healthy thing, however, and the situation certainly made me cautious. Plus, I knew I had kept the Ringtail Gang properly wormed all summer with enough of the appropriate worming medicine. Since that particular liquid wonder smelled like bananas and tasted like bananas, the boys never gave me any trouble about taking their full doses (and wanting more). And by then I was taking my own regular doses of an anti-parasite supplement as well.

Taking Us for a Ride

Besides their much-loved bananas, marshmallows were another huge favorite with the gang. A bag of marshmallows was one of the few things that could stop them in their tracks no matter what mischief they were cooking up. You can bet I kept more than one bag on hand at all times! While it's true that it's not a good idea to feed wild animals (or domestic ones) a lot of human food—particularly sweets—it's kind of like giving your human children a cookie. You know it's not the best thing for them, but you balance their enjoyment of the treat with moderation in all things. Besides, what worked worked! Sometimes I needed the sweet and sticky enticements to ensure the gang's cooperation.

It was a good thing I had a bag of marshmallows handy the day my daughter Dawn was packing her car for a cross-country adventure, because the gang had no intention of being left out of that fun. Those furry gangsters took us for a ride that day, and it was no joy ride (except maybe for them). In hindsight, leaving the car doors wide open while we were trying to pack things—and while the four of them were running around loose at the same time—was just asking for trouble. The two of us were no match for the wily and determined ring-tailed gangsters. As soon as Dawn's bike rack and bike were loaded onto the back of the car, one of the gang climbed on top of the bike and adamantly refused to let go.

"Mom, there's a problem over here!" Dawn yelled to me across the yard. "I can't get on the road with a raccoon hanging off the back of my bike! What should I do?"

"Hold on, I'll get him! Just let me grab a few marshmallows…"

While that gangster distracted us as we tried to extricate him from his perch atop the bike rack, another gangster snuck unnoticed into the backseat.

"Mom, there's another raccoon in the car! Get him out! Get him out!"

"Hang on, this guy's still holding onto your bike rack with all four paws…"

"But this one just found my snacks! Come quick! Mommm…"

Burrowing beneath Dawn's road-trip snacks, the backseat gangster soon got a whiff of potato chips, granola bars, and fruit snacks. Determined to investigate the crinkly packages further, that guy decided there was no way he was giving up his newly taken territory! We had to pay him a huge bribe in marshmallows, plus forking over a granola bar and some chips to get him out of there.

All this chaos didn't even take into account the other two gangsters I knew had to be lurking somewhere underfoot. I felt certain they would enter the fray any second from a third and fourth direction if we didn't get a handle on the situation quickly. It was the biggest rumble with the Ringtail Gang yet, trying to extricate them from on and around Dawn's car when it was loaded down with all sorts of interesting items. By the time we got all the raccoons away from her car and all the car doors shut, I was running mighty low on marshmallows. Dawn didn't have as many granola bars to take along on her trip, either.

The CoonieBear Chronicles

After about a thousand bananas each, the boys in the rafters started to hit puberty. That's not as bad as it sounds with rehabbed raccoons, as long as they live outside by then. Free to come and go as they pleased, the boys started going more often, and for longer periods of time. Eventually, three of them—Sharky, Ducky, and Golden Boy—heard the call of the wild (or the call of available young females) and moved out of our garage entirely. I installed the woods camera far out back and got good photos of the three of them hanging around the feeding station. Clearly, they had now morphed from rehab raccoons into wild ones.

That left one guy, Skeeter, who grew up but not out. He stayed in his Otter kayak all winter. My rehab mentor said it was not at all unusual for one raccoon out of a litter to grow attached to a person and/or place and hang around the first winter. It might be the more needy kit, she said, because kits stay with their mom during that time and he saw me as his mother. She told me simply to enjoy having him around till spring, and then he would likely move on as the rest had. Meanwhile, she advised, I should feed my "failure to launch" guy dry dog food only, to motivate him to be on his way. That would mean stopping the banana fests he loved, and that was a bit of a no-go for me. I was too used to buying red-tape bananas, and too used to enjoying his enjoyment of them. A diet of dry dog food only would be punishment for us both, so I kept the bananas coming.

I was a first-time rehabber then, and as I said, now I look back and realize I could have and should have done things differently. But live and learn! Skeeter became my pal, and our attachment went both ways. I did respect his wildness (or his attempts at it) by going hands-off and no longer handling him at all, for both our sakes. I never again tried petting him or holding him—heaven forbid! More than one rehabber has suffered the pain of numerous stitches as payment for laying hands on an orphan raccoon that has entered puberty. I was never any good with pain, so I kept my hands strictly to myself.

Nonetheless, Skeeter and I became good friends that first winter. We "talked" all the time, and I even posted some of our conversations on Facebook as the "CoonieBear Chronicles," which became briefly famous among my online friends. I realized (most days) that these conversations were all in my head, but I had to do something to pass the long winter, so I chatted the days away with CoonieBear (my pet name for Skeeter).

Finders Keepers

CoonieBear: Could you go get me a boiled egg while I chew up this green thing I found?

Me: Hey, wait a minute! That's my scrub brush. I need it!

CoonieBear: Don't you humans have a "finders keepers" thing? You should keep better track of your stuff. It's mine now.

Me: Give it back, or the next time your water dish needs scrubbing, you're out of luck.

CoonieBear: I can deal with that. I'm a wild animal, you know.

Me: So you're a wild animal, huh? You might want to practice that a little...

CoonieBear: Yeah, I'm WILD. That's what God created me for. And besides, you're making me live outside.

Me: Yet you get your food and water from where?

CoonieBear: That's what God created you for. Stewards of the earth and all that...

Me: Um, wait a minute...there's faulty theology at work here somewhere.

CoonieBear: It works for me! Don't forget that egg. I need to go chew up my new toy.

These "conversations" went on every day that winter, whenever I headed out to the garage to replenish Skeeter's food and water. Northern Michiganders have to entertain themselves somehow during the long, cold winters, and I think I entertained a lot of people with my Facebook-chronicled raccoon exploits. If nothing else, my friends may have been amused by my apparent insanity.

Keeping It Clean

Even our two dogs sometimes became a hot topic in our imaginary conversations:

Me: Hey, *what* are you *doing*? I just gave you that toy! You don't have to drown it in water already!

CoonieBear: Everything is better after it's baptized.

Me: That's certainly true about people. We're better off after we're baptized. I don't think the same applies to toys.

CoonieBear: I've never gotten my paws on anything that wasn't improved by a good dunking in water.

Me: Yeah, but honestly, I think as a species you raccoons have some OCD going on in that area. I mean, it's *three degrees* out here, and now you have everything all sopping wet. You should follow Fritz's example. You don't see him dragging his new toy into his water bowl.

CoonieBear: But he's a *dog*, and everybody knows dogs are a cleanliness-challenged species. Speaking of examples, I could give you a few, like when they lick...

Me: Um, no, let's not go there. Keep it clean! That's what this is about, after all.

CoonieBear: I really don't know how you can stand living with two dogs in your house. You'd be a lot better off letting *me* live with you!

Me: Um, no, let's not go there either, Mr. Wild Animal. We've been down that road before.

CoonieBear: I may be a wild animal, but at least my stuff is clean...

Me: Right. Well then, enjoy your new freezing cold toy.

Not Birds of a Feather

Our resident chickens also got in on the act. Thankfully, raccoons rehabilitated around chickens rarely harm them or even steal eggs. On the bright side, Skeeter followed this pattern. On the dark side, he wasn't above sticking his nose in where it didn't belong, including in the chicken coop. I went out to collect eggs one time and was shocked to discover that not all of the flock that day were birds of a feather. There on the roost was a chubby, furry creature *not* of the egg-laying sort, merrily teetering back and forth next to a couple of bemused chickens.

Quickly, I called to my husband across the yard: "Michael, come see this new breed of chicken!"

"What are you talking about?" he asked.

"It doesn't have feathers, but it has a ringed tail..."

"You're kidding!" he exclaimed.

"Nope. Not kidding!"

The Facebook "CoonieBear Chronicle" went like this:

Me: What do you think you're doing in the *hen house* at high noon?

CoonieBear: You were in the house, and I felt like some company, so I came in. But that *stupid* fence flap above the gate only swings one way so I couldn't get back out. I had to take a rest on this roost instead.

Michael: C'mon, buddy, I have some nice dog biscuits for you if you get out of here. It's strictly off-limits to raccoons.

CoonieBear (ambling out as we held up the flap)*:* Okay, terrific. Listen, that fence flap is going to be a problem for me next time I come in here. Can you fix it so it swings both ways?

Me: Um, we were sort of going on the premise that you wouldn't be coming into the chicken coop to begin with. At all. Ever. By the way, how were the hens for company?

CoonieBear: I gotta say, they're a few eggs short of a dozen.

Me (to my husband): What does he mean by *that*? How many eggs did he *eat*?

CoonieBear: You have to admit, those hens don't exactly function at my higher intelligence level.

Michael (grabbing enough dog treats for our two canines, plus a raccoon): Because you're so smart, I'm not changing the flap. Next time, find your own way out of the coop.

Hens (watching CoonieBear amble away): Hey, how come that big, furry chicken gets to free range today and we don't? No fair!

Prodigal Raccoon

Despite his other daily antics, Skeeter left the chicken coop alone after that incident, which I appreciated—although I think the hens missed him a little. He lived happily in his favorite kayak all through that winter and into the spring. With the warmer weather, however, he

Skeeter, up-close one last time

began to venture farther from home base, as my rehab mentor had predicted he would. Eventually, he strayed by day and by night. At first he was gone for an entire night, and then for two. Then he would disappear for a whole week at a time.

I vacillated between two extremes as our resident raccoon became a prodigal raccoon. At times, I was sick with worry over all the terrible things that could happen to him. After one of his lengthier absences, I was relieved to walk outside and find him hanging out in a roll of fencing behind the garage. I quickly snapped a picture that became my favorite photo of him. That photo also captured the last time I ever got that close to him again.

After that encounter, Skeeter began going up more, as well as out. Most of that second spring of his life he stayed nearby but out of reach, far up in the tall trees around our yard bordered by the woods. Whenever I came out and spotted his furry face up in a tree, he wouldn't hide. But when I talked to him, he wouldn't come down closer to me either. He was getting wilder every day. The more time he spent up and away, the more he seemed in his element living on the wild side. He was finally happy being right where he should be.

Before long, I didn't even catch sight of Skeeter up in the nearby trees anymore. He seemed to have moved farther away from the house and farther back into the woods. That, too, was as it should be. I felt both bereft and satisfied, recording in a daily log entry, "I haven't seen Skeeter in six weeks...he has gone completely wild now and has left me heartbroken but happy for him."

After the final time that I saw him "in person," Skeeter graciously made some cameo appearances in my woods camera pictures. In one photo a raccoon had its fur right up in the lens, so it just had to be him (probably tinkering with the camera). As I let him go in my head and my heart, I knew there would be other cries in the night for me to answer and other raccoon kits to help grow and then let go. It was not by any means the end of my wildlife adventure when he left. It was just the beginning.

5

JUST THE BEGINNING

Do not despise these small beginnings, for the
LORD rejoices to see the work begin.

ZECHARIAH 4:10

It was indeed just the beginning of my adventures with wildlife when Skeeter and the Ringtail Gang fully returned to the wild side. Since then, a number of animals have come and gone at the Lion's Den, my specially installed wildlife shed that now houses much of my rehab caging. Many of their stories are soon to unfold in these pages, including my adventures with Spark and Pigeon George and Jay-Jay and Bunny (not a very original name, I admit) and Frodo. As a rehabber releasing these animals back into the wild, I shouldn't name them at all because it can foster attachment. But most rehabbers end up naming the animals anyway.

Speaking of names, as soon as you walk in the door of the wildlife shed, you'll see a metallic gold-on-black drawing of an incredible lion's head. The drawing represents Jesus as the Lion of Judah and has the words "Be Strong and Courageous" inscribed on it—a reference to Joshua 1, where the Lord tells Joshua to do just that. Each time I walk into the Lion's Den, I thank the Lion of Judah for being with me whenever I care for one of His small creatures.

Depending on the circumstances, animals in need of help come into rehab with a backstory I may or may not know. If only the animals could talk and fill me in! I do my best to figure out what happened to them, with the help of any human rescuers who bring them my way. Then I fix whatever is troubling them as best I can so they can regain their freedom fast and live out their lives in the wild, as they were meant to do.

That is what the rest of my animal tales are all about—the Lion of Judah and His birds and His beasts and me, a simple believer involved in wildlife rehabilitation. I think I am actually the one being rehabilitated as He takes me on this adventure of getting to know so many of His furred and feathered ones. They often make me laugh, and sometimes make me cry, and always show me something new about the intricacy of God's creation.

In the Beginning...

Before I tell you in the next chapter about the adventure I had with an unbelievably tiny spark of life that came in, let's take a quick look at the very beginning of the animals. In the Bible's record, I noticed something interesting about God's creation of the animals. From the beginning, He divided the animal world into three categories, which sets the stage for how I view the orphans I rescue and release and how I relate to them:

> God said, "Let the land produce living creatures according to their kinds: the livestock, the creatures that move along the ground, and the wild animals, each according to its kind." And it was so. God made the wild animals according to their kinds, the livestock according to their kinds, and all the creatures that move along the ground according to their kinds. And God saw that it was good (Genesis 1:24-25 NIV).

Notice that this identifies for us *wild animals*, *livestock*, and *creatures that move along the ground* (which scholars classify as possibly including reptiles, insects, and other such small animals). God Himself put in place these three distinctions among the animals He created for us to enjoy. Keeping this in mind can give us a better understanding of how we humans relate to the animals, particularly to the different kinds.

For instance, I must say that I find wildlife rehabilitation to be a different sort of animal, so to speak, from keeping livestock or having pets. Granted, the Bible tells us that "every sea creature, reptile, bird, or animal is tamed and has been tamed by man, but no man can tame the tongue" (James 3:7-8 HCSB). "Taming the human tongue" sermons aside, the first part of that verse has always fascinated me. Apparently, we humans are able to tame any creature on earth if we put our minds to it (which gives hope to animal lovers everywhere).

Yet obviously some creatures are more easily tamed than others. Taking your cue from those three categories in Genesis 1, I'm fairly certain you would have an easier time taming a kitten that becomes a cat than you would have taming a cub that becomes a mountain lion. Even after a short time working with wildlife, it has become clear to me that most creatures in the wild category have absolutely no interest in being tamed. When I open their cage door at release time, they're gone in a flash of fur or feathers. They might come back now and then to see if I've left any food lying around that they can steal, but they don't come back to stay.

My domestic pets and livestock, on the other hand, act much differently. The canine, feline, and poultry residents around our place have always been happy to eat and stay, and eat some more, and stay some more...and eat and stay again. Not so, the wild things. They eat and run, literally.

This was quite a revelation to me. Until I started doing wildlife rehab, I had never given much thought to how God created the animals in a way that places wildlife in a class of its own. The wild ones just were not originally designed to become close to humans or make good pets. Besides the fact that it's illegal in many places to make pets of them (and should be, for many reasons), did you ever wonder why people don't try to tame them more often? It just isn't a workable plan; that's why! They were specifically designed to be what they are—wild animals. For me, that's part of what makes wildlife rehabbing such a delight. I see it as a rare chance to be around—and even to get my hands on—a whole category of creatures that are otherwise typically out of sight and out of reach.

The Lion and the Lamb

From the time I first noticed that God identifies three categories of animals, I have found it fascinating to think about how we humans relate to them in different ways. I have also found it fascinating that Jesus is identified with both the *wild animal* and *livestock* categories when Scripture calls Him either the *Lion* or the *Lamb*. Revelation 5:5 says of Him, "Look, the Lion of the tribe of Judah, the heir to David's throne, has won the victory." And John 1:29 says, "Look! The Lamb of God who takes away the sin of the world!"

There is no comparison between a lion and a lamb, yet the Savior is called both. That makes sense when you think about it. God created both of these greatly divergent creatures, one a wild animal and one livestock. As different as they are, they can both teach us so much about Christ's nature and character. Thinking about Him as both the Lion and the Lamb has provided me with some powerful insights into who He is and how He operates in my life.

I usually think about one facet or another of the Lion and Lamb comparison every day. Sometimes I think of Christ as *Jesus, Savior, meek and mild*—the Lamb. Other times, I think of Christ as *Jesus, Savior, strong and wild*—the Lion. Both these characterizations comfort me, although these days perhaps the Lion leaps to the forefront more often, probably due to my activities in the Lion's Den. It is there I need His strength and power to help me keep alive the tiny sparks of life that come in. Next up is the story of one of the smallest of these sparks. In fact, that's what I named this terribly unfortunate but terrifically determined little orphan—Spark—in honor of his will to live.

6

THE "SPARK" OF LIFE

Even if my father and mother abandon me, the Lord will hold me close.

Psalm 27:10

Nothing brings more satisfaction than seeing a baby enjoy its milk, whether from its mother or from a bottle. Babies and milk go together. Mother's milk, delivered straight from the mom, is best whatever the species, of course. But in a hungry moment, other delivery methods for the milky nourishment sometimes must do. Once orphan animals are desperately hungry, they soon accustom themselves to being fed from syringes, eye droppers, bottles, or whatever else is handy to help get milk down their tiny throats and into their empty little bellies. I wasn't sure, however, that such would be the case with Spark.

My best guess is that this unbelievably tiny neonate red squirrel was orphaned so early in life that he barely had time to learn how to drink from his mother. I don't believe he had enjoyed very many meals before he got separated from her. He just didn't seem to have a clue about how to go about the business of eating.

"Neonates" are wild babies of any sort that are too young to have any fur or feathers, the true newborns that haven't had much time to grow yet. They look indescribably weird to me, like a blob of pink Play-Doh that is almost—but not quite—shaped into some unidentifiable animal, with dark splotches added where eyes and ears should be.

Even rehabbers need time and experience to be able to identify neonates at first glance, because these tiny ones bear no resemblance whatsoever to the animals they will become. And when they enter rehab, their pink skin, for which they're often called "pinkies," is usually all wrinkled from dehydration, and possibly dirty or damaged to boot. Spark was certainly all of that. My first impression wasn't, *Oh, how cute!* My first impression was more like, *Oh, how ghastly! Whatever that thing is, it isn't going to live long...*

Spark at intake

Pinkies have that effect on you. You're momentarily horrified to see something like that out in the light of day (where it should never be seen anyway). Those kinds of sad and weird-looking little creatures belong safely tucked away in a warm, dark, quiet nest wherever Mom has hidden them. And that's where they need to stay—at least until they look presentable enough to meet the world.

Yet there Spark was, in all his wrinkly pinkiness. His rescuers had looked down and spotted him scrabbling around on the hard pavement of a store parking lot under the blazing summer sun. No trees were nearby for him to have fallen out of; there was not so much as a bush or a patch of grass. It was hot, black pavement only, with that tiny Spark of life in the middle of it. He was a hard-luck case if I had ever seen one.

Miniscule but Mighty

The only way tiny Spark's terrible, horrible, no good, very bad day could have been more disastrous were if a car had run over him. My best guess at his backstory (rehabbers do a lot of guesswork because the animals can't tell us what troubles them) was that he dropped out of the undercarriage of a car or truck someone had driven to the store. Red squirrels are notorious for wreaking havoc in, on, around, and under people's vehicles, as you may already know if you live where they live. It would not surprise me if Spark's mother had built her nest and delivered her babies in the undercarriage of a car. A little nest-shaking over a bump in the pavement was probably all it took to jar Spark out of his happy home so that he was left behind when the car drove away.

Like me, Spark's rescuers had been a little horrified at his pinkie appearance. Still, they took him home and tried to give him a few drops of cow's milk on a Q-tip. He wasn't having it! He didn't know what to do, and they didn't know how to help him. That turned out to be a good thing since cow's milk is such a bad thing for wild babies. Yet these finders were simply being compassionate and trying to keep whatever "it" was alive while they called around to find a wildlife rehabilitator. They brought him in the instant they found someone more experienced who could take him. That kind of rescuer gives orphan animals the best chance of survival!

When these people handed Spark over to me, however, I really did think, *That thing isn't long for this world!* Those are not the words I said to his rescuers, of course. I've seen from experience that God has put an unbelievably strong spark of life in all His creatures, so I figured wherever there's a spark of life, there's hope.

"We'll do the best we can," I told his finders. "Let's start right now."

They watched with interest as I weighed and examined the less than half an ounce of Spark there was. So very tiny! Figuring that most critters' stomach capacity is about 5 percent of their body weight, I knew that meant Spark could only take in maybe half a milliliter (or cc) of fluid at a time. I had an electrolyte mix warmed and ready so I could start rehydrating him as soon as he arrived. He wouldn't nurse from a tiny nipple; he didn't seem to know how. But when I started dribbling the mix a few drops at a time into his mouth from an oral syringe, wonder of wonders he swallowed and swallowed again. We were all smitten at how mightily determined he was despite his miniscule size.

From that moment on, for all his clumsy efforts at feeding, Spark made it clear that he was one spark of life that was *not* going to be put out easily—not if he could help it. He swallowed all the rehydrating fluid I offered, every time I offered it. When he seemed recovered from his dehydration and from any cow's milk that had gotten inside, I gradually switched him over to specialized squirrel formula. With that, he really went to town!

He even learned to love what are called Miracle Nipples, specially made for squirrelly types. He soon learned how to get the most out of them the fastest. He ate like such a horse at every meal that I had to rein him in a little so he wouldn't aspirate formula into his lungs and get sick. Every time I fed him, he would do a little happy dance with his back legs that was ridiculously cute.[1] It was wonderful to see him disappoint my initial expectations that whatever "it" was wouldn't live long, and to see him show such enthusiasm for life and food.

Feeding Frenzies

Spark was enthusiastic practically to the point of having a feeding frenzy at every meal, which was okay by me. If only there had not been so many of those meals to deal with. You can put baby birds and raccoons and rabbits to bed for the night after a final late feeding, but not baby squirrels or opossums. Oh no! Their pinkie forms have to be fed around the clock, which is why rehabbers start looking so haggard as spring baby season gets into full swing.

In the middle of the night, every night, I would stumble bleary-eyed out of my warm bed at the sound of my phone alarm and head downstairs to my bathroom to roust Spark out of his warm bed for a

---

[1] To watch the "Spark doing the Happy Dance at feeding time" video, visit my website at www .trishann.com and click on the "Raccoon Gangs Book" tab at the top. Scroll down to the "Videos from the book" section, where you'll find a dozen videos listed under the drop-down arrow. Spark's happy dance is among them.

meal. (There was no point in keeping him out in the wildlife shed at that stage. He didn't stir out of his nest in a little cage near the bathroom sink, and I didn't want to trek outside in the dark to feed him. Getting up at night was rough enough.) I'd warm up the squirrel formula in hot water and throw another SnuggleSafe heat button in the microwave. (Those are the most indispensable baby animal warmers ever!) Then I'd open the bathroom door, reach inside the cage, and pick up that tiny, hot little spark of life. He'd squirm and squeak a little, and then go to town on his meal. Afterward, I'd clean his face and "restroom" him at the other end.

It took me a little time to figure out the wee hours feeding routine, but I soon got it down to a speedy ten minutes, after which I could crawl back into bed, only to repeat the process at first light. I could sleep peacefully till then, knowing Spark wasn't suffering any hunger pangs. And at least I had company while I was awake. Our dog Fritz has loved babies, both human and animal, ever since we got him, and he has never harmed a living thing. He would sit at my feet for every feeding (day or night) and wait his turn to be allowed to sniff Spark (held safely in my hand) for a second to make sure the baby was okay before I returned it to the nest. Fritz frequently slept by the cage during the day as well, a self-appointed babysitter. (The door was closed by night when I was asleep, of course. Our sleek cat, Satin, was animal baby crazy in a different way than Fritz.)

Prizewinning Feeding Fanatics

As I mentioned earlier, it usually takes a little while for wild animal orphans like Spark to figure out how to feed from a source other than Mom, but most of them quickly get to the point where they are quite enthusiastic at feeding time, if fairly quiet about it. Bunnies and squirrels like Spark are nearly silent, albeit grateful at the moment of milk delivery. Little opossums make only a gentle sneezing sound when hungry, which is a funny and appealing characteristic.

The prizewinning noisemakers of nature at feeding time are baby raccoons. I can't even describe how loudly they can turn up the volume when they realize feeding time is upon them. They give a whole new meaning to the term *feeding frenzy*. That's part of the reason behind their unchallenged reputation as the hardest critters to raise rehab style. At feeding time, grabbing the first raccoon kit out of four or five absolutely guarantees that the rest of them will *screeeech* at the top of their lungs in protest. They all want to eat first. It's the nearest sound to a noise that can drive you insane with only a few minutes of exposure I have ever heard.

I'm glad squirrels like Spark are so much easier to deal with. Feedings with them—even a whole nest full at a time—are almost a soothing experience by comparison, perhaps with the exception of the feeding that gets you out of bed in the middle of the night. But like human babies, eventually they grow up, and it happens faster than you think. It sure happened that way with Spark...

7

SPARK FINDS A FAMILY

Father to the fatherless... God places the lonely in families.

Psalm 68:5-6

Spark drank and drank his squirrel milk, which I delivered and delivered on a regular basis, minus the nighttime feedings once he grew a little bigger under my care. Eventually, he even sprouted some peach fuzz. That was an exciting day for me after looking for so long at his pathetic pinkie self. I'll never forget the sight of his first short, wispy hair sticking straight up on the top of his head. It was the funniest and most welcome sight ever, if barely visible to the naked eye on his naked body.

Soon other wispy hairs sprouted to join it, which made Spark look endearingly comical. Even though it wasn't my first time around the tree with orphan squirrels, Spark was special, maybe because he was by himself and was beating such overwhelming odds. I couldn't help taking pictures like the proud "mother" that I was. Over time his peach fuzz turned into real fur, and what a sight for sore eyes that long-awaited, fiery red fur was when it finally grew in!

It was astonishing to see Spark grow from a dehydrated, dying ember into a flaming red squirrel—an unbelievable transformation. His finders thought the same, as I kept them apprised of his growth by sending photo updates their way. They were some of the most involved and interested finders after the fact that I had ever known, which was both wonderful and unusual. We all agreed that Spark's transformation was miraculous. The way God designed every creature to grow and reproduce after its own kind is miraculous anyway! Whenever I rehab any animal orphan, watching that growth process close up always feels like a miracle to me.

Rattle, Rattle, Bang

You'd think having one very tiny red squirrel squirrelled away in a little cage in my bathroom would be a relatively quiet affair, but you'd be mistaken. It was quiet only at first. Spark's transformation from newborn to toddler was nearly as noisy as the Ringtail Gang's. He was simply a tornado on a smaller scale. Once he got his paws under him and figured out how to use them to climb up and down the bars of his cage, the *rattle, rattle* of his speedy movements was almost constant whenever he was awake. Around and around his little cage he would go, and when I added a few tree branches going every which way, his delight knew no bounds as he practiced his balance and even a few tentative jumps (not tentative for long).

Now that he was running around outside his cozy nest so much, I had to keep the bathroom door shut day and night. Otherwise, the temptation to sit and watch Spark was too overpowering for poor Satin the cat, whose posture clearly told me she was hatching plans to break into the cage and break out the squirrel—and not with any good result. I increased my vigilance, and so did Fritz. He plopped himself down by the bathroom door and did a fair job of keeping the cat at bay.

Meanwhile, the *rattle, rattle* coming from behind that closed door was turning into a *bang* on a regular basis. Spark started to push and pull on everything in his cage, rearranging his little world to suit himself. He was also making it abundantly clear that his little world was starting to feel too confining. His behavior reminded me of those old Westerns where the jailbirds grab their tin cups and run them over the bars of their jail cells, setting up such a clatter that it drives the sheriff crazy.

In addition to his stunning physical growth and development, I could almost see a mental growth spurt taking place behind Spark's bright little eyes. He was still drinking formula, but only a few times a day, and he often preferred to lap it up himself from a little dish rather than sucking it from a Miracle Nipple in my hand. Although he still loved his spot of milk, his taste for being treated like a baby was diminishing every day.

The Priceless Payoff

On release days, I have to say that the payoff on my rehab investment is priceless. To stand at the squirrel cage out in the woods, open the door wide, and watch nearly grown youngsters like Spark get excited over scrambling up and down a tree trunk for the first time in their lives is a sight worth seeing. The excitement is just...squirrelly.

Alas, I didn't get to share that kind of excitement with Spark. Not to worry; as far as

Spark curled up in my hand

I know, nothing as yet has extinguished the fiery young red squirrel Spark has grown into. But when he was old enough to open his eyes and ears and start scampering around, I knew the time had come for me to let him go in an unusual way—to another rehab facility. Like many orphans, red squirrels do much better raised and released with others of their own kind. Most seasons when I get in a singleton like Spark, other red squirrels soon follow, so I had never had to raise one alone. That had been true every season until Spark. He came in by himself, and no other squirrel calls followed. That meant I needed to get creative about networking with other rehabbers in order to give him the best chance of survival.

Spark was a late-season baby, born at the tail end of the summer, almost into the fall. The later into the fall it became, the less likely it was that another singleton red squirrel would come my way. Sure enough, by the time Spark was ready to work on his squirrel socialization skills,

I was still second-squirrel free. That meant I needed to call other rehabbers to find out who else had baby red squirrels and what we could arrange to foster Spark's next growth stage.

To my relief, another facility not impossibly far away had a small litter of late-season reds similar in age that would make excellent adopted siblings. So once the energetic Spark of life I had raised fully developed from a ghastly pink blob into a gorgeous specimen of a red squirrel, I loaded him up and made the bittersweet trip to the other rehab facility to hand him over.

To my delight, once I got Spark where he was going, I found out the facility would be overwintering him and his new siblings for eventual release in the spring. That was more than I had dared hope for! Overwintering requires extra staffing and a wintertime cage setup much larger than I have at the Lion's Den. This facility was well suited to overwinter wildlife and was caring for several other squirrels that were also too young for a fall release. I didn't get to see this squirrel zoo firsthand because I dropped Spark off at the intake office, and the different litters were spread throughout volunteer foster parents' homes. But his new foster parent sent me a picture of Spark thriving in his new digs, which I appreciated because I know how busy parenting squirrels can keep you.

Spark and I had hit the jackpot with his new arrangement. Release day would come for him the next spring, but I didn't mind at all spending the winter thinking about how he would pass the cold-weather months safely indoors in the company of his adopted siblings. They would stay warm and well fed by their human foster parent, all without having to face the rigors of a Northern Michigan winter while still so young.

I knew that by the time spring came around again, Spark would be more than ready to go out and light his wild world on fire, and he wouldn't have to do it by himself. I wouldn't see that payoff moment personally, but I have enjoyed the fun of releasing enough juvenile red squirrels near the Lion's Den to imagine what it would look like. Everybody's adrenaline, human and animal, is always off the charts when release day comes around. I could easily imagine the fireworks Spark and his pals would cause when their cage door was first opened to the outside world. The excitement would be positively contagious![1]

Squirrels like Spark that I've released myself spend their first few minutes racing sky-high up into the trees like the wild and free things they suddenly are. Then they often come back down to home base, sit on top of their cage, and look at me with bright, happy eyes (or so I imagine). The fun thing about squirrels old enough to release in the fall (besides the fact that they're so much easier to rehab than raccoons) is that they'll return to the release cage again and again, and maybe even spend the winter living inside it with the door left ajar if the location is protected enough from the weather. Then I can stop by often and drop some treats for them, knowing they're not starving their way through their first winter out in the wild.

We call that supplement feeding, where we drop food every day or two as a way of seeing those inexperienced, motherless types through. We don't do it often enough or in large enough quantities that they can live off it without lifting a finger, so to speak. We want them to be motivated to hunt and gather for themselves. But we drop enough so that they don't starve or suffer in a rough weather patch, especially if they didn't have the time or know-how during good weather to stock up on winter provisions for themselves. That is often the case for released juveniles, so supplement feeding helps.

The red squirrels, which are the squirrel species I most often rehabilitate, sleep through some of the cold weather, but certainly not straight through. They stay quite active all winter. And seeing them day to day in the wild makes the payoff priceless for me. Even simply seeing their tracks in the snow here and there and everywhere around the cage tells me that my rehabbed, released critters are doing just fine. That puts some spark in my life on the coldest winter days!

---

[1] To watch a fun "Red Squirrel Release Day!" video and catch the excitement for yourself, visit my website at www.trishann.com and click on the "Raccoon Gangs Book" tab at the top. Scroll down to the "Videos from the book" section, where you'll find the release day video under the drop-down arrow. You'll also want to watch the "First Taste of Freedom" video that you'll find there.

8

PIGEON GONE BAD

*Just ask the animals, and they will teach you. Ask
the birds of the sky, and they will tell you.*

JOB 12:7

I never planned to become a pigeon fancier. My husband never planned to become a pigeon's first love. George swooped in with his own set of plans.

He did not swoop in, actually. Nothing so grandiose or graceful. He was unceremoniously dropped off in a cardboard box. Some well-meaning friends found him walking down a busy road one day, not far from a car-flattened co-hatchling that looked just like him and was probably from the same nest. These friends figured he was in trouble and knew I did wildlife rehab, so they scooped him up, named him George for some reason, and brought him our way. He may or may not actually have been in trouble, but now that he was in our lives, we were the ones in trouble. We just didn't know it yet.

Honestly, George was the homeliest thing I had ever seen. (Or almost. It's hard to look worse than a neonate pinkie, but he came close.) You know how something can be so ugly it's cute? He was not that. Not by a long shot. He was just plain homely, with his little yellow fuzzies sticking up all over his body and his massive, misshapen-looking beak. (It wasn't misshapen, but it sure looked it.) Have you ever seen a nestling pigeon? They're kind of scary looking. If they were a hundred sizes bigger, they would be shoo-ins for starring in monster movies. And you have to feed them by shooting goo down their throats.

I had not dealt with a pigeon before George. It took a while to learn to feed him properly. It took a lot of peas, too, which oddly is

Pigeon George at intake

one food that suits baby pigeons nicely. Their parents feed them crop milk—a secretion from their crop lining (an enlarged part of the esophagus) that both pigeon parents regurgitate straight into their hatchlings' mouths (another odd thing about them). It's mighty hard milk to reproduce, but peas are a handy substitute, along with some baby bird food slimed down with water into the requisite gooey consistency and delivered via a syringe without a needle.

George loved it all, peas and gooey food alike. He feathered out splendidly into a kaleidoscope of color. He grew and grew. He was ungrateful, whereas I had been kind of hoping for some gratitude. He did not fall in love with me, even though I worked so hard to take care of him. He fell in love with Michael. He just could not get enough of my husband. My theory is that they were thrown together too much. As George was fledging and spending time learning to zoom around the yard, my husband was redoing the siding on our old farmhouse. (It looks great now, although it would look even better if he had let *me* choose the color. But that's an issue for another day in a book on marital accord, or discord.) Michael spent hours every day outdoors, working on the siding. Consequently, George spent hours every day adopting him as a surrogate parent. Never mind the hand that was feeding him.

So George fell in love, and Michael found himself in a love/hate relationship with a pigeon. How could anyone not love the beautiful bird a now-older George had become, with his snow-white body and his blue, green, and iridescent purple trim feathers? How could anyone not hate the way George landed on Michael every time he came out of the house? George bit his ear for fun and dive-bombed everyone who dared get near enough to my husband to talk to him. George was not about to share his first love with anyone else.

Getting the Last Laugh

We and our misguided pigeon/lovebird soon became the laughing-stocks of our friends and neighbors. But once George targeted them for reprisal, they usually stopped laughing pretty quickly, while George got the last laugh. People had to admit that George made an excellent guard pigeon, and a general deterrent to unwanted—and wanted—visitors.

Alas, my youngest daughter ended up among those visitors we wanted around but whom George did not. For some reason clear only to his little birdy brain, he took a particular dislike to Dawn—much to the frustration of my new son-in-law, who has since been known to talk of nefariously doing away with said guard pigeon.[1]

Pigeon George is an excellent example of wildlife rehabilitation gone wrong. They say a bird in the hand is worth two in the bush, but I don't know about that anymore. I could not get George to head out into the bush so we could decide. I called a favorite rehab mentor and asked her (begged her) for advice. I told her we thought that maybe we could take George downtown where other pigeons lived and release him amongst his own kind, but I did not want to do that without her input. It is easy to condemn rehabbed animals to death by starvation or predation if they are not released properly into a suitable environment.

George foiled our plans again, as did my mentor. When she was growing up, one of her close relatives had kept pigeons, and she laughed until she cried when she heard my tale of woe. "Of course you can take him downtown and release him," she said. "Take him anywhere you want! But he's a pigeon that has basically grown up at

---

[1] To watch an amusing "George guards the door!" video in which Pigeon George strongly suggests that Dawn (the camera person) takes a hike, visit my website at www.trishann.com and click on the "Raccoon Gangs Book" tab at the top. Scroll down to the "Videos from the book" section, and when you view this one under the arrow, wait for what George does right at the end!

your place. As soon as you release him, he'll take off for home and possibly beat you back to the house!" (Why was this reminding me so much of the Ringtail Gang? They beat me home too. Juvenile wildlife is so delinquent.)

"Are you kidding?" I said. "But wouldn't he want to stay with his own kind, look for a mate, and raise a family?"

"Sounds to me as if George already has a mate. He chose your husband! He'll come right home to him," she told me. "Just be glad it's a pigeon and not something worse."

What does she mean by that? I wondered. *I hope I never find out...*

"Pigeons are great fun and perfectly legal to keep without a special permit," she added. (I could still hear her chuckling in the background.) "And it sounds as if *George* has decided to keep *you*. I think your husband has himself a personal pigeon pal for life."

We tried a couple of times to give George a new love interest by buying him some pals from a "pigeon farm" that raised birds for shooting practice (poor things, but at least the price was right at five dollars each). We had high hopes for our matchmaking schemes, but they never quite panned out. One bird took off for its old home despite all our efforts to follow expert advice and acclimate it properly to its new home. (It wasn't going back to a promising future.) A couple of other birds we bought hung around for good, but they turned out to be males! (It seems sexing young pigeons is nearly impossible even for many pigeon experts.) That scenario of inadvertently bringing in some competition didn't go over well with George at all, so we have since stopped trying to become pigeon matchmakers and have resigned ourselves to letting him run his own love life.

Who Wears the Pants?

George came in for rehab in August, somewhat late in the season. There was no way he was leaving our place for life on his own before his first winter hit. As I said, there was no way he was leaving our place at all, as far as he was concerned. That's how I went from being a wildlife rehabilitator to being a pigeon fancier—or at least being a pigeon keeper. Fancier was a bit of a stretch.

Cold weather came along, and George took to sitting on top of our porch light by the door for warmth. My husband simply could not stand sitting in the warm house and wondering if George might be too cold. Before I knew it, George was in the house a lot, sitting on the back of Michael's office chair.

Chatting with Pigeon George

Really? I thought. *Isn't there enough for me to clean up already with the rehab critters outside and the domestic critters inside?* I wasn't happy about cleaning up pigeon poo in a formerly pigeon-poo free household, so my husband came up with a plan. He built that bird a warm and dry pigeon condo right outside our door. It was gorgeous! I would have lived in it. And he attached it right to the side of the house, next to George's favorite porch/pigeon warming light. George could hop back and forth from the top of the light into his straw-filled, windbreaker condo anytime. He loved it! He slept in it every night, but only after turning around and around in it several times while cooing his unceasing delight.

I can't say visitors to our household were equally delighted by the new arrangement of having George live just above our main entryway. He soon took it upon himself to fiercely defend his territory. Heaven help the people who came along and reached up a hand toward his pigeon condo in fascination, exclaiming "What a beautiful bird!" Their very next exclamation was always a mortified "*He bites!*"

Sure enough, he bites. Still does—usually me. But only when I put my hand anywhere near him without grasping him firmly, keeping all my exposed skin well out of reach of his beak. He doesn't break the skin, thankfully, but he has become quite the expert at grabbing hold and pinching. Most of the time it happens when I am filling his food bowl (the ingratitude).

To my consternation, the fact that George now had a pigeon condo to call home did not keep him out of our home. Somehow, both he and my husband had taken a liking to him being inside with us. He was more of a regular visitor than most of our friends (or former friends) who had run afoul of his self-appointed sentry duty at the door. So somehow, even though he had a fancy home just outside the door and a personal warming light, I was still cleaning up pigeon poo. Something had to be done.

Pigeon pants. That had to be the answer.

Is that a real thing? you ask.

It is. I direct you to Google, where I searched to see if I could find a solution to our pigeon problems. Sure enough, I googled "pigeon care" and up came a pigeon-and-dove rescue organization website. Sure enough, those exist too, even though George had ended up at the Lion's Den instead of one of those. The website I looked at kindly included a section titled "What Are Pigeon Pants?" Therein, I read that rescued pigeons unreleasable into the wild make passable indoor pets, especially if they are wearing pigeon pants. (Are pigeons wild? Are they domestic? I don't know. Neither does George.) For me, that whole idea begged the question, What am I supposed to do with a rescued, *releasable* pigeon that simply prefers to be indoors? But there was nothing much to help me there.

The pigeon pants, however, come in myriad designer fabrics and colors, so that was helpful to know. None of them were cheap, mind you. Who knew that there was such a market for fashionable pigeon clothing? You outfit your bird in style, put a piece of paper towel or a tissue in the specially made beneath-the-tail pocket, and no more messy poo dots your furniture! The pants contain it all. Wonder of wonders, each pair of pigeon pants even comes with a little loop attached and a soft leash so you can take your indoor pigeon outdoors for a walk and not lose it. For me, that begged another question: But what if I *want* to lose it?

This and other pigeon sites assume that you want to outfit your pigeon in pants and have it in the house with you. Truly, this concept had never occurred to me, and at first I brushed it off as silly. Who would want to do that and pay fashion designer prices for the privilege?

It turns out we would. It didn't take too much more cleaning of poo before I decided that pigeon pants were absolutely the most brilliant invention I had ever heard of. I chose a bright blue pair that I thought would match our bird, forked over my credit card number and address, and waited by the mailbox. One momentous day, the pigeon pants arrived. They were really something, although I didn't know whether to laugh at their unusual appearance or cry at the price on the invoice. But now at least I had a plan I thought would work well for everyone involved. I hoped George would be as impressed with it as I was.

Not so. Have you ever tried to put pigeon pants on a nippy pigeon that does *not* want to wear them? At all. Ever. To my deep disappointment, our adopted pigeon made it clear that he would *not* be adopting my new plan. He also made it very clear who wears the pants in this family. He does—at least figuratively.

I still have the pigeon pants in their original package, and I take them out and admire them once in a while. George never gives them a second glance. To this day he "wears the pants," but he is never going to wear the pants.

9

FLYING IN UNDER THE RADAR

The LORD is a shelter for the oppressed, a refuge in times of trouble.

PSALM 9:9

Rehabbing wild birds is a tricky business. There are magnificent moments of success, offset by moments of equally stunning failure (hi, George). The feathered ones themselves are a tricky combination of fierce and fragile. They come with this fierce determination to fly free, offset by this weird fatalism that can cause them to die shockingly quickly of capture myopathy—the stress of confinement and/or being handled by humans. They don't want to be touched by a big, scary monster in human form, no matter how well-intentioned the monster is, and they don't do well with pain. I am a lot like that myself, so I sympathize.

I know you probably don't think you're all that scary, but to a wild bird you and I are the stuff of nightmares! Not that I have the chance to become very many birds' worst nightmare. Between federal rules and regulations and the Migratory Bird Treaty Act (MBTA), the kind of birds I can rehab is limited. The laws are a good thing that I don't object to. I just have to mind my p's and q's, or the regulations can become a nightmare. Birds of almost every kind are highly protected, except for non-native, nonmigratory species like European starlings, house sparrows, and feral pigeons (hi, George). Anyone is free to become involved with those birds. But the rest of the feathered population is strictly hands-off unless you obtain a federal permit to have those birds in your possession.

Obtaining such a federal permit is not for the faint of heart. I won't go into all that is involved, but look it up sometime. I admire whole-heartedly the bird rehabilitators who succeed, and I'm glad to have some of them within driving distance of my place, which means all these federally protected birds that need help have somewhere legal to go. That's a very good thing for me, and for them.

I don't fly in the face of any regulations on purpose, of course. I wouldn't dream of taking in a fierce raptor or a member of a waterfowl species, all of which require highly specialized care. And your average songbird is also hands-off, thanks to the MBTA. Every once in a while, however, something flies in under the radar...

The Blue Beggar

Enter Jay-Jay. Some kindhearted people wholly oblivious to the strict songbird regulations had found this sorry blue jay pre-feathers and post-falling out of his nest. Then they couldn't find either nest or parent to return him to, so they raised him themselves on who knows what.

I have to say that despite the issues involved, they did a fine job of it. Baby birds need an exacting diet to develop properly. The vast majority of the time when someone tries to raise one and doesn't know the ins and outs of how to do it, the nestling either dies or grows up sadly deformed. Not Jay-Jay! Somehow these finders did things mostly right, and he grew into the most stunning and energetic blue jay fledgling I'd ever seen.

Jay-Jay's rescuers had no idea what to do with a fledgling that was no longer content to cuddle inside a little nest, and they certainly didn't want to let him go in their neighborhood full of cats. So I got the call—this in the days before we had any federally permitted bird rehabbers nearby. He couldn't be released so young in a yard full of cats, so I told them to bring him to the Lion's Den and I'd take a look at him.

Jay-Jay arrived at my place in fine feather. His every move showed off a color palette of gorgeous blues, and in the way of blue jays he was both appealing and demanding at the same time. Jays sometimes get a bad rap for being the bullies of the bird world, and I can understand why. But nobody can argue with the sheer beauty and personality they put on display! While I almost hesitate to admit this in public, they've been at the top of my favorite bird list for a long time. There was no way I could resist Jay-Jay. As a rehabber I couldn't responsibly leave him in these people's possession, and I certainly couldn't send him back to Catville, so I took him on.

My plan was to see what I could do about getting him into a rehabber's hands somewhere (hours away) who had the proper permits, and I would have made the effort. But as it turned out, it wasn't necessary. He had grown to the point where he was too big, strong, and restless to be confined to a cage, so I let him go in the cedar trees next to our

Jay-Jay at intake

ancient barn/garage where the Ringtail Gang had lived. It's the perfect spot for fledglings or for birds that just need a little feeding and recovery time from minor mishaps. We feed wild birds out there every day, and the barking of our dogs in our fenced yard keeps area cats far away. The dogs are so used to our chickens that they don't bother wild birds either, and a predator on the hunt has to really want a bird badly to face off with those two crazy canines.

Since Jay-Jay was no longer in a cage at our place, he was no longer technically in anyone's possession. Technically, therefore, no songbird regulations were being violated. That didn't stop him from possessing us! As a fledgling he needed frequent feedings from his "parents," and he let us know that he expected us to step up and fit the bill. Or fill the bill, if you want to get technical about it—his bill, a lot, and often.[1]

---

[1] To watch "Jay-Jay," a video of me working hard to get Jay-Jay to feed himself, visit my website at www.trishann.com and click on the "Raccoon Gangs Book" tab at the top. Scroll down to the book videos, and you'll find Jay-Jay there.

Which we did for weeks and weeks, the whole thing exacerbated by the fact that, true to form, Michael couldn't resist building Jay-Jay a perch of his own on the nearest cedar tree. As you can imagine, Pigeon George was not about to share his private condo with a noisy, rambunctious little interloper that probably reminded him too much of himself at that age.

Jay-Jay loved his new perch and immediately claimed it as his feeding station. We kept a bowl of fledgling-tempting foods like fruit and seeds on it at all times, out of which he could easily have fed himself. Yet he much preferred that we step out of the house and feed him whenever he called. Which we did a lot because he called a lot. If we weren't home to feed him, he would go to our neighbor across the way and beg for a feeding there, which also happened a lot (good thing our neighbor was a willing jay-sitter).

We didn't mind Jay-Jay and his antics, although he and George had such similar personalities that the two of them at once could be a bit overwhelming. If Jay-Jay didn't call for a feeding at regular intervals, one or the other of us would step outside and call him. His response was to wing his way in at full screech and check out whatever treats we had in hand—unless he was over at the neighbor's. Then I would go retrieve him yet again with abject apologies.

A real bonus was that our resident wild blue jays were usually in and around our bird feeders all day, and Jay-Jay could watch them closely and interact with them. He learned about being a blue jay in the wild by watching blue jays in the wild, all while being fed by us and protected by our dogs. He had the best of both worlds.

Eventually he grew almost as wild as his wild blue mentors, and he needed us less and less. Soon he started winging his way off on his own more often. But to this day, whenever a raucous blue jay swoops into the yard, lands unusually close, tilts its head in that blue jay way, and vocalizes loudly in my direction, I'm pretty sure it's Jay-Jay. In fact, I think he was here just yesterday.

Forget My Feather Fetish!

You may wonder why the rules are so strict about having anything to do with songbirds, even the common ones. I wondered that myself, so I looked into it. It's our own fault for having a feather fetish. The Migratory Bird Treaty Act I mentioned was enacted more than a hundred years ago, in 1918, because back then people were killing too many birds so they could use the feathers to manufacture things such as fashionably feathered hats. Numerous species were soon facing extinction because of this out-of-control fetish for bird fashion, so something had to be done.

The MBTA was the result. This law has been updated a little since 1918, but not very much. It is so complex that the U.S. Fish and Wildlife Service has a special website, called the Feather Atlas, to help you and me determine whether a feather we see on the ground is legal to pick up and take home or not.[2]

Most of the time, it is *not*. That's the level of protection birds now enjoy. I am not talking eagle feathers, either, which many people know require a permit to possess. I am talking about almost any feather! There are some bird exceptions (hi, George), but for the most part, we had better *not* collect feathers beyond those of our own chickens. I'll quote you a short section of the MBTA:

> It shall be unlawful at any time, by any means or in any manner, to pursue, hunt, take, capture, kill, attempt to take, capture, or kill, possess, offer for sale, sell, offer to barter, barter, offer to purchase, purchase, deliver for shipment, ship, export, import...transport...carry or cause to be carried, or receive...any migratory bird, any part [including feathers], nest, or egg of any such bird, or any product...composed in whole or part, of any such bird or any part, nest, or egg thereof...any person, association, partnership, or corporation who shall violate any provisions of said conventions or of this subchapter...shall be deemed guilty of a misdemeanor and upon conviction thereof shall be

---

2 For more information from the U.S. Fish and Wildlife Service's Feather Atlas, visit https://www.fws.gov/lab/featheratlas/.

fined not more than $15,000 or be imprisoned not more than six months, or both.[3]

Check out those last few lines again. Serious stuff! You can be tried, convicted, fined thousands of dollars and imprisoned for months for badgering a migratory bird, much less for possessing any part of it. I realize that feathers are beautiful and remarkable, and when you find them in nature you can study them and take pictures, but it is almost always illegal to take them home. Thankfully, the online Feather Atlas puts the MBTA regulations in somewhat simpler language:

> The possession of feathers and other parts of native North American birds without a permit is prohibited by the Migratory Bird Treaty Act (MBTA). This protects wild birds by preventing their killing by collectors and the commercial trade in their feathers, and extends to all feathers, regardless of how they were obtained. There is no exemption for molted feathers or those taken from road – or window-killed birds.[4]

Feathers have always been one of my favorite things, but since finding out more about the MBTA, I have reined in my feather fetish. Nowadays, I might look at a blue jay feather under my bird feeder or a sea gull feather on the beach, and I might even run a finger along it to feel its beauty firsthand. But then I do the lawful thing and leave it where it lies.

Likewise, I stick to the birds and mammals my rehabilitator license allows. I'm glad birds are so well protected. It has made a huge difference in the number of birds we have left to enjoy. Yet at first it also made rehabbing more of a challenge because for so long I didn't have

---

[3] To read the MBTA in more detail, you can visit this website and also obtain a copy if desired: https://www.fws.gov/le/USStatutes/MBTA.pdf. The quote comes from the U.S. Codes 703 and 707 sections.

[4] "Feathers and the Law," *The Feather Atlas*, U.S. Fish and Wildlife Service, last modified February 28, 2020, https://www.fws.gov/lab/featheratlas/feathers-and-the-law.php. The Feather Atlas home page also provides links to interesting information on a wealth of bird-related topics, including how to identify feathers via multiple scanned images. Visit https://www.fws.gov/lab/featheratlas/.

any bona fide bird rehabbers nearby. I did, however, have birds nearby that kept flying in under the radar...

The Early Birds

Enter the "Early Birds." A huge number of red-breasted robins, Michigan's state bird, had migrated back to the Mitten State too early one spring and had then found themselves in deep trouble because of deep snow. Red-breasted robins are heralded all over Michigan as the first sign of spring, but this time their timing was off! Blown around by a mid-April blizzard, these early robins started falling to the ground in droves. And people all over our county started calling me, upset at finding robins dead or dying in their yards.

These good-hearted robin lovers were desperate to rescue the weak, starving birds that hadn't already died. Yet people could not be expected to take the risk of transporting birds from our locality to a properly licensed rehab facility hours away during whiteout weather conditions. I couldn't take the risk either. Part of the expressway leading to the proper rehab location was closed due to the weather warnings, so travel was simply out of the question.

I had to do something, however, so under the 48-hour Good Samaritan clause I took in whatever weakened robins people called me about. Meaning I could have the birds in my possession for a short period of time, provided I was making every reasonable effort to place them into licensed care. With the wild weather there was no way to make such a reasonable effort, so I housed them locally in the Lion's Den.

I got some heat lamps going to ward off the cold, and I provided the birds with good food and rest. My hope was that by the time the storm had passed, the robins would be sufficiently recovered to be releasable right in my yard. Otherwise, I would have to make plans to transport them to properly licensed rehab care after the storm.

To stem the tide of birds flying in under the radar, I also quickly posted online that people could feed the struggling robins in their yards—options that were more affordable than expensive earthworms from the corner gas station. Raisins, Craisins, and berries atop the snow all appeal to hunger-crazed robins, and even shredded cheese that can look like worms to them. Lots of enthusiastic responses came back, so I know people were doing their best to help these Early Birds live through the storm.

On a happy note, the robins that people braved nearly impassable local roads to bring me, perked up just fine after being fed and warmed in the safety of the Lion's Den. I released all of them (and all of their feathers with them, in deference to the law) as soon as the snow passed, which it did quickly—Michigan weather being so capricious. The released robins happily flew the coop (or the Den, rather) much stronger than when they arrived, and I got to watch them merrily pulling worms out of the ground just a few days after I thought they were goners for sure!

Bird in a Box?

Before we fly away on another animal tale, I should mention why you may one day have a bird in a box on your hands. If you are acting as a Good Samaritan, as I did with the Early Birds, you won't need a permit to pick up a songbird in distress. Yes, you should plan to take it to a rehabber as soon as possible, if needed. But it isn't always needed. People come upon downed birds all the time; you have probably done so yourself. Some of those poor creatures just need to become a "bird in a box" briefly, and then be set free.

Bird in a box? you wonder. Let me explain. Songbirds sometimes inadvertently bang into things like windows as they fly around, or things like cars bang into them. Sometimes it's a glancing blow and the bird soon recovers. Other times, the downed bird needs somewhere dark and quiet to catch its breath and shake it off. It needs to be a bird in a box.

If you come across a stunned songbird on the ground, and it doesn't have any obvious injuries, put a cardboard box over it and give it anywhere from half an hour to a couple of hours to recover. Glance at it briefly every half hour, and when it seems alert and lively again, lift off the box and let it go. You have probably just saved its life!

Not to mention that you helped the bird stay in familiar territory, which is best for it, and you saved yourself a trip. If you had put the temporarily stunned bird inside a box and had driven it to a rehabber immediately, it may have surprised you both and flown away as soon as the box was opened. Birds recover fairly quickly from glancing blows.

If your bird in a box hasn't recovered in the span of a few hours, it will need to go into rehab. Collisions and window strikes can be very injurious for our feathered friends. It's not just that they bonk their heads on a window, see stars for a little while, and then recover like some critter out of a cartoon. If only it were that amusing.

In reality, the windows of our houses and businesses are a huge issue for birds. Windows are often positioned in such a way that they reflect the outdoor sky and scenery back to an airborne bird. Even with its bird's-eye view, a bird cannot always tell there is a window directly ahead and may bang right into it.

The Delicate Dove

Enter the prettiest ring-necked dove (aka Eurasian collared dove) I have ever seen. Its golden-brown feathers and soft-looking eyes were positively mesmerizing.

When the call came in, the finders sounded so sad: "We have a beautiful dove on our hands, and we don't know what to do with it. From inside our house, we heard it strike a window with a big *bang*. We ran out and found it lying motionless on the ground, so we put it in a box to give it a breather. It has been several hours, and it hasn't recovered at all!"

"Bring it over," I said, "and I'll examine it." (Again, this was before we had a federally permitted bird rehabber near enough to intervene.) They brought the little beauty to the Lion's Den as soon as we hung up, hopeful to the point of tears that I could do something for it.

"I'll do everything I can," I assured them when they arrived, "but I'm so sorry to say that the prognosis for such a severe window strike is really poor. You did everything right, giving this dove a dark, quiet place to rest after it took the hit and then bringing it in for more help as soon as you saw it was necessary. There's nothing more you could have done! But I'm not sure there's anything more I can do either. We'll see what transpires."

I don't like telling sad stories, but window strikes are a huge part of the difficult side of rehabbing. What transpired with the beautiful but unfortunate dove was that it passed on. Almost as soon as I saw it, I knew it would. It had apparently broken its back in the crash and was paralyzed. It had no movement in its lower half whatsoever, and no movement came back over time. I had to call the finders the next day and report that there had been no recovery for their soft little bird in a box.

Birds are so strong but so delicate, so fierce but so fragile. They seriously injure themselves because they are winging along as happy as larks and don't recognize the danger reflected in that clear, shiny glass. Then they hit a window at breakneck speed—literally. If these hard strikes survive at all, they either die by inches in the wild, or some poor rehabber takes pity on them and helps them wing their way more quickly into the great beyond. (That's mighty difficult too!) Lighter strikes, however, can and often do recover after a brief time-out as a bird in a box.

A Word of Warning

I should give one word of warning: You don't want to pop any old bird in a box, especially the bigger birds. It's worth noting that acting as a Good Samaritan for some kinds of birds can cause undue human pain and suffering if you are unwise about it. Even little songbirds have beak and claw enough, as I can tell you from painful experience (hi, George). They *will* defend themselves when they're not too busy dying of fright, so it pays to be careful.

Be aware, as well, that non-songbirds like raptors and waterfowl are in a category all their own when it comes to self-defense. There are herons with strength enough behind their long beaks to skewer a skull. Loons, as classy as they look, will aim for an opponent's (or rescuer's) eyes when frightened, and they excel at hitting their target. Any rehabbers I've seen handling these species are suited up in protective eyewear and other such gear.

Then there are the raptors, in yet another class all their own. Eagles, owls, hawks, and other birds of prey can inflict pain with beak and talon that you haven't even dreamed of, with hundreds of pounds of pressure behind every nip and grip. I know of an injured owl that sunk its talons through someone in multiple spots, and that's not an isolated incident. Expert bird rehabbers can handle those big, fluffy raptors with consummate skill, but it's a skill people surely better have down pat if they decide to mix it up with birds of *that* feather. The rule I live by is don't attempt to put those kinds of birds in a box. Call for well-trained help instead!

Warding Off Window Strikes

Back to the songbirds for a moment. Having window strikes happen around your place is painful for both the bird and its finders. In the United States alone, it's estimated that between 100 million and 1 billion birds a year die from window strikes, depending on where you get your statistics. Either number, and every number in between, is horrendous.

Did you know, however, that something can be done to those bird-attracting windows to let birds know when it's time to veer away? I keep decals, stickers, or painted hearts from the grandkids on my windows to ward off the birds in flight and help keep them alive to sing and fly another day.

We can all help increase the songbird population by doing such simple, inexpensive things about this one issue. Google "bird window strikes" online and you'll find all kinds of additional solutions. You'll then have more songbirds around to watch and enjoy because simple efforts like that pay off big in preserving these winged wonders!

10

CRAZY CALLS ABOUT CRITTERS

Call to me and I will answer you, and will tell you
great and hidden things that you have not known.

Jeremiah 33:3 esv

Wildlife rehabilitators get dozens and dozens of phone calls, texts, and messages online, often daily, about critters in crisis. Because there are so few rehabbers, the contacts come from miles and miles around, at all hours of the day and night. So be patient if you are calling a rehabber and it takes a little time to get through or get called back, especially in the busy baby season. Some rehabbers even take classes that deal with the volume and variety of calls because it can become so overwhelming.

Some calls result in an animal coming into rehab, and some don't. Even if rehabbers don't take in the particular animal, most will gladly take the time to provide information so rescuers can find appropriate help for their critter crisis. Season after season, the wide variety of calls that come in never fails to surprise me. Animals of every sort get themselves into all kinds of crazy situations, and there are so many compassionate people out there who want to help, even if only by calling a rehabber for advice.

Here is a sampling of the calls I have received over the past few seasons. Some are funny, some are poignant, some are informative, and I think all of them are interesting.

No Finger Snapping Allowed

Caller: Hello, I just pulled off the highway to rescue a snapping turtle. It was going to get hit by a car. Now what?

Me: Are you in a safe location, away from speeding traffic?

Caller: I'm well off the road. Can I drive this snapper to a better place and let it go?

Me: Well, first, *keep your fingers away* from it! And second, turtles need to be released as closely as possible to right where you rescue them. They *do not* do well transplanted elsewhere. They're really nature's homebodies, and they often die if you remove them from their home territory, because instead of settling in, they'll keep trying to get back "home."

Caller: No problem. I see a pond right near the spot where I picked up this turtle. It was probably trying to get there. Shall I take it over to the pond?

Me: Sure, but *keep all your fingers* while you do it! By the way, how's the smell? Snappers can be quite pungent...

Caller: It's terrible! But I love turtles. I can't help stopping for them whenever I see them by the road.

Me: You and my husband both. He's a self-appointed turtle crossing guard everywhere we go. Thanks for caring!

Holy Squirrel!

Caller: Hello, we have a little squirrel that keeps running around in our church. What should we do?

Me: Can you see it now? How big is it?

Caller: It's out of sight at the moment; I think it left the building.

Me: How often does it "come to church," and what does it do there?

Caller: Every now and then it reappears and runs around, usually upstairs in the church balcony.

Me: Maybe it's getting in and out under the building's eaves somehow. You need to find its point of entry, make sure there aren't more young squirrels up there, and block off the opening. Try live trapping your squirrel and putting it outside if it keeps coming to church. Call again if you need more help. It sounds to me as if your "holy squirrel" loves being in the house of God!

Joining the "Pouch Pickers"

Caller: Hello, I just rescued a little baby opossum on the road. It was near its dead mother, but I don't see any others.

Me: Did you check inside the mother's pouch for more?

Caller: I did! But there was "nobody home." This is the only one, and Mom isn't playing possum.

Me: Did you know this officially makes you a "pouch picker"?

Caller: What on earth is that?

Me: Google "pouch picking" sometime, which is a real thing lots of people do in the spring whenever they see a dead opossum on the road. These people keep rescue supplies in their car and check every dead opossum they drive by, rescuing the babies. Pouch pickers are determined people, believe me. I think you just joined them.

Caller: I guess I did, even though it's my first time. I just knew I had to stop the car...

Me: It turns out that you live right near one of my rehab friends. I'm too full of raccoon kits to take an opossum, but we can check with this other rehabber. Your little baby should be with others of its own kind. We'll find it a place.

Caller: That sounds good!

Me: Thanks for caring enough to rescue it. Some of the tiny "pinkie" opossums people find are hard to save, but many older ones can be raised and released successfully. You're giving this one a good chance at life!

Help! "He" Just Laid Two Eggs!

Caller: Hello, remember when I called you about that baby bird last year and told you I thought it died? Well, it didn't. We kept it all winter, being careful not to make a pet out of it. We were sure it was a boy, and we really were going to release it this spring! But "he" just laid two eggs on the bottom of the cage, and now we don't know what to do!

Me: So "he" didn't die after all, and "he" just laid two eggs? Apparently, this bird has taken you by surprise twice now. Let me call the songbird rehabber who has a federal permit and find out what to do next. I'm glad you want to do the right thing and release it now. I'll get back to you.

Dive-Bombings Delay Grocery Shoppers

Animal worker: Hey, one of us got a call from that grocery store in town. There's a sea gull dive-bombing customers at the door and wreaking havoc in the parking lot. Every agency that the manager has called says they can't touch the bird since it's a federally protected species. Got any ideas?

Me: I was at that store the other day and didn't get hit in the head by a sharp beak, but next time I go grocery shopping I'll be especially careful! I can put you in touch with a new bird expert not far from here who has a permit for rehabbing birds and waterfowl. I'm sure she'd know whom to contact for help—maybe the U.S. Fish and Wildlife Service.

Animal worker: The store needs to contact somebody to find relief for some very scared shoppers! It's a little bad for business. We'll contact this bird person and pass the information on to the store.

When my daughter and I went grocery shopping the next day, a "sea gull intervention" crew was up on the store's roof. I hope they had been brought in as the result of a call to that bird expert for advice. Maybe the sea gull had a nest of eggs or had hatched babies up there. I'm not sure what steps the crew took to solve the problem, but by the time we got out of the store, things seemed considerably quieter in the skies above the parking lot. Customers no longer needed to fear a dive-bombing gull.

Kits or Cats?

Caller: Hello, I have two five-week-old kits here with upper respiratory issues, and they really need a foster mom to bottle-feed them! I work and don't have time.

Me: Okay, what happened to the mother raccoon? Was she hit by a car? What else can you tell me?

Caller: No, these are *kitten* kits. You know, the *cat* kind.

Me: Oh, I love the *cat* kind of kits! But I'm sorry; I can't take them. The state asks rehabbers never to mix wildlife care with domestic foster animals. Let me give you the number of the local animal shelter.

Raccoons or Kids?

Caller: Hello, there are four baby raccoons in my kids' tree house, and I want them out. I put up that tree house for my kids, not for raccoons!

Me: I can understand that. Any idea if the mother raccoon is around? It would be best if she moved the babies out herself.

Caller: I don't think she's alive. There was a dead raccoon just down the road, although I don't know for sure if it was the mom.

A baby-faced raccoon visitor

Me: We need to make sure the raccoons are really orphaned. Is there any way you could watch for the mom to come back for a night?

Caller: I have a woods camera I could set up to see if any big raccoons go in or out of the tree house at night. Would that help?

Me: That's brilliant! Do it! Thanks for caring enough to make sure the mom is really gone.

The next day...

Caller: No momma raccoon climbed into the tree house at all, and the babies are screaming with hunger.

Me: Bring them in; they're orphaned. Looks as if I'll have another Ringtail Gang on my hands!

This caller was really clever about using a woods camera to check if momma raccoon was still around. Setting up a camera in an unobtrusive spot is an excellent way to figure out whether wildlife babies are truly orphaned. It can prevent a person's "kidnapping" them from a temporarily absent mother, whose life would then be in danger from mastitis.

Cats Plus Raccoons

Caller: Hello, my outdoor cat gave birth to kittens not long ago, and now there's a little raccoon coming into the yard and nursing from her belly every day. What should I do?

Me: Wow, if that raccoon kit is coming right into your yard, hungry enough to nurse off your cat, it's probably an orphan. That must be some kind of mother cat to adopt a raccoon!

Caller: She's a great mom. But I'm a little worried about that raccoon staying around or maybe even hurting the kittens as it gets bigger.

Me: It's smart to be cautious, with distemper and raccoon roundworm and the like. It's better for both cats and raccoon to get the raccoon to a rehabber and let it grow up with its own kind for eventual release. I'm full of raccoon kits already, but let me give you another rehabber's number who has room.

A Deep Well

Caller: Hello, there's a skunk stuck down in my window well that can't get out. I don't want to get too close and get sprayed...

Me: Right you are! You won't want to scare or startle the skunk, or you'll be wearing a new fragrance! But skunks get stuck in window wells a lot.

Caller: What can I do to help it?

Me: Take a piece of plywood, a ladder, or even a sturdy log, and angle it down in there. Then back up quickly! The skunk will climb out on its own once you've left the area.

Caller: I never thought of that! Seems like a simple solution; I'll give it a try.

Later that day...

Caller: The plan was successful, and all without nasty skunk spray spurting everywhere. Thank you for the idea!

Me: You're welcome. What a relief for both skunk and human!

An Entry for Every Season

Finally and inevitably, every year my Lion's Den phone call/contact notebook has the same entry, made around the same date, just as spring folds into summer and the wildlife rehabbing season kicks into high gear. It goes like this:

Me: Far too many phone calls/contacts are coming in every day now to keep up with writing them all down. No time! I need to go feed the bottle babies...again!

CAMEO SHOTS AND COMICAL LOGS

The earth is the LORD's, and everything in it.

PSALM 24:1

Woods cameras are wonderful at capturing cameo shots of wildlife that you and I otherwise might not get to see. I got our Stealth Cam (one brand, although there are others) as a birthday gift for my husband so he could track the movements of deer out back. He used it less than he thought he would, however, so he regifted it to me to keep track of my released rehab beasts.

I load batteries into the Stealth Cam, strap it to a handy tree, and let it do its thing while I stay inside, warm and dry. It will take pictures or videos, and we enjoy both. The discoveries I make from a single night's worth of photos are both fascinating and reassuring.

Discovery #1: No bears are currently hanging around the supplement feeding area toward which I angled the camera. (Very reassuring! I won't think about any angles the camera isn't capturing.)

Discovery #2: All four of this year's released juvenile raccoons are still alive and are looking fat and sassy as they play around in the weather creek and wade in the pond. (Very reassuring! Yes, I can usually tell my current season's charges from other raccoons, either by their size and unique facial features, or by the distinctive ring patterns on their tails.)

A positive identification naturally gets harder the longer they are out and about on their own.)[1]

Discovery #3: The fox that recently ate six of my chickens is still in residence and also looking fat and sassy. (Not so reassuring!) It's a good thing I had a baker's dozen chickens to begin with, or I'd be out of eggs for sure. But wow, what a gorgeous animal the well-fed fox is![2]

Discovery #4: Again, no bears are currently hanging around the supplement feeding area toward which I angled the camera. (Again, very reassuring!)

Discovery #5: The area's resident porcupine apparently gets the supplement feed all to itself when it comes around. No other animals are ever within sight of it. (Who can blame them?)

Discovery #6: What is that? Good grief, could it be a lone wolf moving through the area, which happens now and again? (Not at all reassuring! Some people who saw this cameo shot thought it was a large coyote instead, but several wildlife people who watched it voted wolf.)[3]

Discovery #7: Aha! Still true that no bears are currently hanging around the supplement feeding area toward which I angled the camera. (Still very reassuring!)

Discovery #8: This year's Ringtail Gang apparently has made the acquaintance of last year's Ringtail Gang or some wild-born raccoons. All eight ring-tailed beasts in the cameo shot are looking fat and sassy.

Discovery #9: The barred owl (no dummy, and very majestic) is haunting the trees just above the pond where many dinner-sized critters come to drink. This owl will answer me when I call. (I made that

---

[1] To watch a "Ringtail Gang on release" back by the feeding station video, visit my website at www.trishann.com and click on the "Raccoon Gangs Book" tab at the top. You'll find this gang in the book videos.

[2] To watch a "Chicken stealer eats watermelon for dessert" video, visit my website at www.trishann.com and click on the "Raccoon Gangs Book" tab at the top. You'll find the chicken stealer in the book videos. Now that I'm watching the video again, I'm not sure it's watermelon that the fox is helping itself to, but at least the chicken stealer is enjoying something else I provided—other than chickens!

[3] To watch the "What Is It?" video and decide for yourself whether it's a small wolf or a large coyote, visit my website at www.trishann.com and click on that "Raccoon Gangs Book" tab at the top, and then scroll down to the book videos.

discovery one day by hooting at it in a poor imitation of its distinctive barred owl call, but it acknowledged my efforts anyway.)

Discovery #10: And one more time, no bears are currently hanging around the supplement feeding area toward which I angled the camera. (And always *very* reassuring!)

And so it goes with the woods camera. As soon as a wild animal crosses the sensor, the camera captures a cameo shot or a video far more entertaining to watch than TV. Sometimes I position the camera by the little drinking pond, sometimes by the squirrel cage, sometimes by the raccoon feeding station, and sometimes in the old orchard that the deer dearly love. Then all I have to do is retrieve the SD card on one of my walks and pop it into my computer. Instantly, we can see who is doing what and where out in the backwoods. The woods camera gives me an even bigger window into the fascinating world of wildlife, a window I never tire of looking through.

Laugh-Inducing Daily Logs

Delving into the pages of my daily animal care logs is another way to get a quick and often funny peek at what goes on in and around the Lion's Den. I keep daily logs for a number of important reasons, and they differ from the call logs in the previous chapter because they detail the animals I actually take in. They cover every wild animal every season, recording their care and feeding from intake all the way to release and often beyond. The entries are useful for future reference, should medical or other questions arise about either the humans or creatures involved in the different scenarios. They also refresh my memory about what worked and what didn't with certain species, ages, and stages, and they help me document the statistics necessary for the yearly reporting requirements in my state.

Beyond the practical reasons for keeping daily logs, going back and reading through them provides me with some laughs after the fact. There are a fair number of sad or difficult moments that come any rehabber's way when dealing with wild animals in crisis, so I find it especially encouraging to take time to celebrate the successful moments and laugh at the comical moments.

Nothing makes me smile as much as going back and reading about the "live and learn" lessons the various gangs of baby raccoons have taught me over subsequent seasons. They alternately surprise, delight, and dismay me at every turn. There seems to be no end to the raccoon species' quirky little personalities, as the following log entries show.

Raining Raccoons Again, Season 2

June 30

Intake today: an almost three-pound male raccoon kit between two and three months old, "Ringtail." I can't say much for the originality of his name, but I can say these people have had him too long. I'm glad they're finally surrendering him to a rehabber. They've gotten Ringtail completely used to being handled—spoiled even. But he seems healthy enough, if a little too happy to be around humans.

Imagine rescuers letting a raccoon hang out on their kitchen counters! Not something I would do now that I know more about zoonoses—diseases transferable from animals to humans. Sorry this guy came in alone, especially since he's so used to hanging out with people. He will be lonely...

July 1

Ringtail will not be lonely after all. Intake today: an almost three-pound male raccoon kit between two and three months old, "Thief." His name is an apt description of just about any raccoon anywhere.

Same situation as yesterday: Thief lived in the house with his rescuers, slept on the dog bed, ate with the family. I hope they and their pets are still healthy! On the bright side, he seems healthy and has been under their observation long enough to pass the distemper quarantine, the same as Ringtail. So these boys are together already, play-fighting like lunatics. They will be so good for each other.

July 8

Today's intake after a one-week break: a barely two-pound female raccoon kit around two months old that I've named "Goldie" because her fur is so blonde. I think she might actually be a rare blonde raccoon. She's so gorgeous.

Lots of eye appeal here, but not exactly a warm or welcoming disposition. Goldie is what rehabbers call a "grumpy"—a baby that comes in completely wild, snarly, snippy, and nippy (and in this case, full of fleas). Goldie made it clear from the get-go that absolutely no warm fuzziness is allowed between us. In fact, she has earned herself the nickname "Fruit Loop" with me because she's so crazy. This one will be a challenge. She intimidates me instead of the other way around.

P.S. Poor Michael! My husband will soon be the fruit loop if this rainstorm of raccoons keeps up.

Goldie the Grumpy

"You just have to wrap grumpies tightly in a towel, like a vet wraps a cat," says a mentor when I call her in dismay about trying to feed grumpy Goldie. "Then you bottle-feed them by force until they realize you're not out to kill them but to nourish them. Then they will relax."

Goldie shows no sign of relaxing, other than when she's watching Ringtail and Thief at play in the cage across the room. I'll keep her cage within sight of theirs and then pop her in with them as soon as her distemper quarantine is over. The boys can deal with Miss Grumpy! They certainly seem interested in doing so. They're spending a lot of time girl-watching across the room these days!

Goldie came in off the side of the highway, where she was in danger of being hit by a car. She seems to hate humans, which won't be all bad come release time. I won't try to win her over; I'll just take care of her till she can take care of herself.

Last One in Is a Rotten Egg

With all these raccoons raining down on us and growing up so fast, Michael and I finally decided to dig the pond we've been thinking about for a few years. The effort was Herculean, even using his heavy equipment. It was dastardly hot and mucky. But oh, the looks on the raccoon kits' faces when they first approached the new pond on a walk and realized it was a swimming hole. The fun they had made all our efforts worthwhile!

We even put planks up between the trees in a sort of overhead walkway system above the pond, so rehabbed raccoons could go back and forth from tree to tree. And Michael installed a wooden feeding platform up there as well. Now I can toss supplement food up there, and the raccoons can come and get it without ever coming down within reach of the larger canine or feline predators (coyotes, wolves, bobcats, even cougars—Northern Michigan has them all). This is going to work so well!

Meanwhile, Goldie is helping the boys learn how to behave more on the wild side, and the boys are helping her be just the tiniest touch more civil in captivity. She won't have to be civil for long (which I define as not trying to bite my hand every single time I feed her). These three will soon go on full release back by the new pond, where I think they'll live very happily.

The raccoons playing at their new pond

Coon-Free Comical Logs

Not every Lion's Den log entry involves raccoons, although raccoon kits certainly seem to have taken up the bulk of my rehabbing time and effort so far. What follows are a few entries about some of my more memorable non-raccoon visitors.

Bubble Trouble

Intake today: three tiny squirrels from a veterinary practice north of the Mighty Mack. That would be Michigan's Mackinac Bridge. A vet tech brought these down and across and says they've been nose-bubbling formula, so pneumonia is a big concern. I'll feed them s-l-o-w-l-y with a small Miracle Nipple rather than a syringe, which I hope will end the bubble trouble.

A mentor tells me the esophageal opening where milk goes down a baby squirrel's throat has the same diameter as a small paper clip. No wonder it's hard to get formula into them without it spurting out their noses or going down into their lungs! She also tells me that when nose bubbling happens, I can cover a squirrel baby's nose and mouth with my mouth and suck out any extra formula so it doesn't enter the lungs. (Note to self: As disease-free as squirrels generally are, that particular rehab trick probably is *not* happening here.)

It turns out these babies are red squirrels, which is fine as long as I release them far enough back in the woods that they don't reappear in the yard and build nests in our car's air filter, which for some reason irks Michael. All three are eating very well now. There's no reason they shouldn't survive and thrive, even without mouth-to-mouth (and nose) assistance from me.

Bird Trouble Begins

Intake today: a pigeon fledgling [yes, the infamous Pigeon George you met in an earlier chapter].[4] This fledgling is two-thirds the size of an adult but still wants to be fed substitute pigeon milk [crop milk] by mouth, along with peas. This fledgling wants to be fed a lot. A lot of peas. A lot of formula. This fledgling knows what it wants, and it wants it a lot.

---

[4] To watch a video of "Fledgling George," visit my website at www.trishann.com and click on the "Raccoon Gangs Book" tab at the top. You'll find little George in the book videos, and you can also watch a video of "George at bath time" as he takes a cool shower on a hot day under the backyard pump.

[And later] Now that George is taking in seeds and other foods, I am beginning his "soft release" by day out near our bird feeder. No need to wait because he came in almost ready.

George is definitely enjoying his free flights! But he wants back in the cage at night. Did I mention George likes to land on my head? It turns out spikey talons and soft scalp are not the best combination.

Squirrel Family Reunion Fail

Intake today: a squirming ball of seven(!) almost pinkie red squirrels that an animal shelter volunteer found had been unceremoniously (and probably unknowingly) dumped on the ground at a huge fundraising sale. The mother squirrel apparently did not travel with the babies to the site of the sale.

The volunteer knows the yard where the box of sale items with baby squirrels buried inside first originated. I'll warm and rehydrate them and take them out there to see about reuniting them with Mama. Maybe she's looking for them around a nearby tree and will retrieve them from underneath. It's worth a try!

[And later] No squirrel mom came to retrieve the babies, although they were left safe, warm, and accessible under a tree all afternoon. No point in leaving them there since squirrel moms won't retrieve babies after dark. Looks as if I'm taking them home again. They came in so dehydrated and chilled. How are the weakest ones even hanging on to life? Two are not doing well at all.

Update on the "Squirrel Ball"

A rehab mentor described to me how orphan squirrel babies will form a "squirrel ball" when they're cold. She said the babies sleeping on the outside of the ball get more chilly than the rest and can develop pneumonia more easily. This mentor has also never rehabbed any squirrel babies this small and says to keep on as I am doing, rehydrating and feeding them, but not to be surprised if some of them don't make it. (Note to self: At seven feedings a day times seven tiny babies, plus a night feeding, somebody had better survive—or more than one somebody—or I'm going to be a little put out with the squirrel world!)

[And later] Only a few of the almost pinkies made it all the way to release, but that isn't a bad outcome, considering that they all were nearly dead on intake. It was not an easy process for the surviving orphans or for me, but they've grown up into glorious-looking red squirrels that are doing very well post-release. I see them all the time when they come down to the open release cage for food. Although they are all but wild, they know me enough to come say hi from afar and grab a quick bite to eat. Lovely outcome! I'm delighted with them.

Repenting of a "Pet" Opossum

Intake: the cutest juvenile opossum ever, which the rescuer made a temporary pet. In the rescuer's possession for a whole month, it was bottle-fed and then weaned. The rescuer learned what to do from online articles and took the little critter along everywhere, even to work. But now the realization has hit that in captivity this opossum will never enjoy the life it should, plus it's illegal to keep one without a permit. Getting a permit is complex (as is long-term adult opossum care), so the rescuer has determined that surrendering the opossum to rehab would be best for everyone.

Fuzzy little opossum at intake

Oh, the pain! The rescuer cried and cried on dropping off this opossum baby that had become such a close pal. I did my best to emphasize the excellent care it would get in rehab, but I felt sorry for the finder.

How could I not? I know what it feels like to be closely involved with a wild animal baby and then have to let it go.

[And later] This young opossum was an absolute hoot—one of the cutest creatures I have ever rehabbed.[5] Still sympathizing with its rescuer, I would have loved to keep it around myself, but instead I transferred it to a rehab facility a few counties over that specializes in opossums. They have other juveniles in residence that they will over-winter for a spring release. Their current residents will make great pals for this one, which will do very well with its adopted siblings.

Dog-Pulled Squirrel Tail

Intake: a juvenile red squirrel with a really sore tail end! Some-one sent me a Facebook message about this squirrel, which a dog had caught by the tail. Its tail had been pulled so hard that the poor little thing couldn't even walk after the rescuer retrieved it from the dog.

There are no obvious injuries to the squirrel, but it is very reluctant to move or walk much. I'll keep it under observation for a couple of nights and see what transpires. Now we wait to see if its tail end is just sore or if there's a more significant injury.

[And later] The little tail-pulled squirrel is back to full movement after a couple of days of rest. So glad he will be fine! To my delight, another juvenile red squirrel is coming into the Lion's Den, a healthy one that can keep Sore Tail company as neither should be released alone. I'll give them a few days to make friends, and once they figure out that the release cage is "home" if they want it to be, I'll open the door and let them set their world on fire, as red squirrels certainly are prone to do.

[And later still] That's it; they're free! I released the two red squir-rel youngsters out back today. You should have seen their excitement as they zipped up and around and down the trees right next to their cage. Their zest for life is unparalleled. I'll supplement feed them peri-odically. You have to love seeing pine squirrels, another name for reds,

---

[5] To watch a video of this temporary guest, "Mini opossum enjoying grapes," visit my website at www .trishann.com and click on the "Raccoon Gangs Book" tab at the top. You know where to find the mini opossum…under the book videos arrow.

living far back in the piney woods where they belong, as opposed to getting into trouble by tearing up people's attics or building nests in car filters. Just hearing their high-pitched chatter when I walk in the woods makes me smile.

GOING DOWN A RABBIT TRAIL

Let your "Yes" be "Yes," and your "No," "No."

MATTHEW 5:37 NKJV

Someone called me in great remorse one spring over a small bunny that was left orphaned and hungry. "A tree was being cut down, and when it fell, it landed smack on top of a bunny nest!" this distressed caller exclaimed. "The falling tree killed this bunny's mother and every one of its siblings, so it's the sole survivor."

"Bring the bunny over, and I'll take a look at it," I said.

"Do you think there is anything you can do for it?" the person asked. "It's small but seems uninjured. We sure hope it survives. The person cutting down the tree had no idea there was a nest of bunnies in the way, and we all feel terrible about what happened!"

"I'll do all I can, but you should know that in spite of their huge numbers, bunnies often don't do well in rehab. That probably seems surprising when you see so many rabbits hopping around outside. But a lot of rehabbers won't even take in baby bunnies because their low survival rate gets depressing. I'll take this one anyway and do my best with it, as long as you understand that it may not live."

"Understood! We'll be right over," replied the relieved caller.

To Rehab or Not to Rehab?

Not to go down a rabbit trail, but a fair-sized debate among rehabbers is whether or not it's worth trying to rehabilitate wild baby bunnies. The bunnies don't thank us for any sort of intervention into their secret little lives!

Young babies with their eyes still closed are especially hard to rehabilitate. Mother rabbits manage to raise them by the millions, so you wouldn't think it would be so hard. Yet rehabbers who don't specialize in rabbits are looking at only a 10 percent rabbit survival rate. For many rehabbers, a 50 percent rabbit survival rate overall would be considered a really, really good result. So the question becomes, Is it worth the time, energy, and resources needed to take care of little rabbits?

I don't have a definitive answer to that, which doesn't stop the bunny calls from coming in fast and furious, almost as numerous in spring as the rabbits themselves. I decided that, in spite of the bunnies'

Bunny at intake

sorry survival statistics, I should take a 12-hour online course in rehabilitating rabbits from a large and successful rehabbing facility to see if I could up my percentage of survivors. The course covered everything you could think of, from feeding newborns to making sure juveniles get enough natural light to produce vitamin D. It was intense and involved. It was also kind of funny that when all was said and done, the instructor's concluding remark was along the lines of "You can try to do...[this, that, and the other], but in the end, young bunnies are just very hard to rehabilitate!"

That much I already knew. Bunny babies are so cute, but it can be so hard to keep having the buns you take in be fine at one feeding and stiff, cold, and *gone* the next. All the same, I couldn't help feeling sorry for this lone survivor of the tree disaster. I had rabbit formula on hand and the know-how to relieve its immediate hunger. I had the caging to keep it warm and protected. I even had some tips from the online bunny class that I was hoping to put into practice. Besides all of that, I had already named the little one Bunny, albeit not very creatively. Once you name an animal in your head, it's pretty much too late to refuse to take it in. Live or die, this orphan bunny was coming my way.

Coming Out on Top

I can't even describe the sweetness of holding a silky soft baby rabbit, and this one was cuter than any Easter bunny picture I'd ever seen! Thankfully, Bunny was already eyes open, ears up, and furry—all important developmental milestones since the older a bunny is when it comes into rehab, the better its chance of survival. Plus, of all the pinkies out there nesting in the wilderness, bunnies are far and away the ugliest. On days 1 and 2 of a neonate bunny's life, before it grows any fur, it looks for all the world like a dark and tiny hippopotamus. The first time I held one, I had no idea what it was. I was relieved that Bunny was well beyond that stage, probably between one and two weeks old.

From the start it surprised me that Bunny would even take in the milk I offered. Rabbit orphans often have to be tube-fed, which is effective but still no guarantee of ultimate survival. It is an awkward feeding method. But this bun was eating from a syringe for me right away and was enjoying it.

Bunny grew quickly and didn't bloat on me (succumb to gastrointestinal tract stasis), which is a huge issue for these little ones. The things I had learned in the online class were paying off in that regard. I was using distilled water only. Even though our well water tastes wonderful to humans, the minerals in it can damage delicate bunnies' digestive systems. Their inner workings develop so quickly that it's impossible to duplicate the gut bacteria, enzymes, and other factors that must stay finely balanced for them to negotiate that speedy growth. Hoping to ward off internal issues, I supplemented Bunny's diet with a probiotic powder other rehabbers had used successfully. In Bunny's case, an ounce of prevention was turning out to be worth a pound of cure.

Even more satisfying, Bunny and I were somehow managing to negotiate the tricky changeover from formula to leafy greens, which is the crucial weaning period most rehab rabbit babies don't survive. Trying to provide the right greens in the right amounts at the right age (from about the second week onward) is the stage where things often go so wrong. You'd think popping a little pile of fresh-plucked green grass in front of a young rabbit would do it. Or giving a bunny lettuce or spinach from the fridge. But those greens can actually be disasters for its gut during this transition period. I learned from the class to search for exactly the right kind of wild foods wild bunnies grow up eating, at least in our locale—dandelion greens, white clover, ribwort plantain, and lots of crabgrass (aka goose grass), which turns out to be good for something after all if you're a bunny rehabber.

I hoped providing these four specific greens in the right amounts would make all the difference. I pulled them up anywhere I could find them, cut them into bite-sized niblets, misted them with distilled water for moisture, and popped them into Bunny's cage in a huge pile. Then I held my breath to see what would happen.

Why a huge pile for such a small creature? Because a little pile won't do! I learned from my bunny course that if you have two or three bunny weanlings in a small cage, to provide enough nourishment for them you have to fill the cage *up to the very top* with moistened greens. When they eat their way out from underneath that monster pile, it's time to do it all over again. Good thing these greens are so easy to find. Each baby bunny consumes between two and three cups a day, which keeps rehabbers busy scouring their yards for "feed weeds."

I piled Bunny's greens fresh and high every morning, and Bunny mowed down every pile. Thriving so well, Bunny soon was able to move into a roomy wire hutch outside during the day. The hutch had no floor, so it sat directly on the grass. For added security, I moved the upside-down cardboard box that served as Bunny's sleeping quarters into the hutch, too, but Bunny rarely hopped inside. Clearly, the feeling of grass underfoot (or underpaw) was a novelty too delightful to miss.

Bunny stretched and rolled and lippity lopped around the new enclosure blissfully, often nestling down in the tall grass and soaking up the sunlight with just some ear tips visible. I spent a lot of time soaking up the sight from a distance, doing my best to avoid startling Bunny, who was fast learning to enjoy the great outdoors as a wild rabbit should.

At night I put Bunny back into the Lion's Den to thwart any predators, and each morning I moved the

Bunny graduates to the release cage

floorless hutch to a new location in the yard before popping Bunny back inside. Letting this little one forage for greens at will was a huge relief after all the time I had already spent hunting and gathering them.

Living on such rich fare, Bunny soon stopped drinking formula altogether and likewise was becoming more skittish all the time about my presence. When I had a hard time catching Bunny to bring inside at night, I knew it was time for the next transition. I dug a ready-made rabbit hole in the ground next to the wildlife shed and popped the whole wire hutch over it. Then I propped up one edge on a brick so Bunny could move in and out of the hutch freely or pop down the rabbit hole to hide or to rest. After that, I left everything alone, other than keeping a sharp eye out for telltale rabbit movements around the yard.

Bunny moved into the rabbit hole the very first day—exactly what I hoped would happen. I left the hutch propped over the top of the hole for another week or so, and then I moved it out of the way. At about a third the size of an adult rabbit, Bunny was growing quickly and didn't need that kind of cover anymore. From time to time after that, I would often see a young rabbit I'm sure was Bunny hopping around the yard.[1] The other day, I even caught Bunny meandering around in our old garage/barn, gleefully cleaning up the spilled birdseed around the storage bin. "Momma" didn't raise no dummy!

When the Answer Is No

For me, taking in sorry little Bunny was a wildlife intervention worth attempting. Yet the answer is not always yes to the question "To rehab or not to rehab?" This question gives rise to a fair amount of debate in some quarters about whether wildlife rehabilitation itself is worthwhile. People ask, "Wouldn't it be better simply to let nature take its course in most cases?"

I don't have a definitive answer to that question either. Public opinion runs the gamut. On one extreme you have the belief that *we must try to save every animal, no matter the time, effort, money, or danger.* On the other extreme is the belief that *nature should always be allowed to take its course, and any form of human interference is harmful.*

As I grew more involved in wildlife rehab, I had to consider where I would place myself on that spectrum. As it turns out, I think the answer is both *yes*, we should do it, and *no*, we should not—on a case-by-case basis. Sometimes we can prevent or relieve a lot of animal suffering by stepping in with a compassionate *yes* and intervening in a case like Bunny's. Sometimes there's room for wisdom that would cause us to step back with a *no* and let nature take its course, for the best resolution of an animal's situation and perhaps to protect human health and safety.

---

[1] To watch "Rabbit on release," a video of a young rabbit about Bunny's size here that I later managed to rehab and release (and also catch on camera, although it's not easy since they're shy and speedy), visit my website at www.trishann.com and click on the "Raccoon Gangs Book" tab. Then scroll on down to "Videos from the book."

A "Surfeit" of Skunks

Enter a "surfeit" of skunks...that's a *no*. The longer I engage in wild-life rehab, the more I realize that the best balance between the two extremes of *yes* and *no* comes in knowing which answer to give when. When a call came in from a frustrated person whose old outbuilding was serving as a roof over the heads of a whole family of skunks, *no* was my answer.

"Hello, I think there's a litter of eight little skunks living under an old building on my property. I don't know what to do about it. I don't want them under there. Can you come take them away?"

No! There was no way I was going to go out and personally hand a whole passel of skunks an eviction notice. Actually, a whole passel of skunks is called a *surfeit*, which, according to Webster's, is a word that means "disgust caused by excess." If you think about the odious odor these animals can emit, that name for a passel of them makes perfect sense. It didn't make sense, however, for me to take on a surfeit of naughty skunks.

"I'm sorry," I told this caller, "but I can't do that. For one thing, we rehabbers can't spend our time driving around to remove what people call nuisance animals, because then we would never have time to rehab the other animals we have in our care. For another, because skunks have been confirmed to carry rabies in this state, Michigan rehabbers are not allowed to take in any of them. I understand your frustration at having a whole litter of skunks nearby, but if I want to remain in good standing as a rehabber, I can't intervene. And you shouldn't interfere with them, either. This is one time where we need to be strictly hands-off. Do you think for some reason that these skunks are orphans?"

"No, they look to be in pretty good shape. They're very active. I probably just haven't seen the mom yet, or maybe they're old enough to be out and about on their own already. I guess I understand the reasons why you can't come get them, but is there anything that can be done? I'm not looking to hurt them, but I'd like them to move on!"

I thought about that for a minute, feeling compassion not just for the skunks but also for this poor person stuck with an outbuilding full of them. "It's really best in this case to let nature take its course," I answered. "But you just might be able to speed up the process. There's a lot of information online about how to carry out what's called a *humane eviction* of unwanted wildlife—without endangering yourself or the animals. If you google humane eviction, sites like urbanwild -liferescue.org will suggest numerous things you can do. For example, I know you can play a loud radio in the building the skunks are living under, and hopefully the noise will drive them crazy enough to move on. You can leave a light on out there, and you can put out some safe, nontoxic items with odors they hate. Make the area where they're living a whole lot less appealing to them, and perhaps they'll leave of their own accord."

The caller really liked the ideas I shared. "That's brilliant!" he said. "A humane eviction—I never thought about trying anything like that! I'll look it up and give it a try."

The ideas I gave that caller have worked for a lot of people who find unwelcome wildlife living at uncomfortably close quarters. Humane evictions are just that—humane. They basically let nature take its course—with a little prodding—but they avoid endangering the animals. More importantly, they are meant to avoid endangering the people as well. I know I felt safer in this case by not putting myself in close proximity to a surfeit of skunks—and no doubt I could breathe easier too!

THE DIFFICULT DAYS

The LORD keeps you from all harm and watches over your life.

PSALM 121:7

A s lighthearted and fun as raccoon gangs, pigeons gone bad, and other amusing aspects of wildlife rehabilitation can be, I would not be giving you the whole picture if I didn't talk about dealing with the more difficult days. I have found it best to face the issues that come with wildlife rehab head-on with courage, calmness, and conviction—not that I always succeed at those at any given moment.

It's not unusual for rehabbers to give up because of the weightier issues involved in working with wildlife. According to an International Wildlife Rehabilitation Council (IWRC) class I took, the average amount of time a rehabber lasts from getting his or her first permit or license to quitting completely is seven years. After only seven seasons, the average rehabber has had enough.

I don't blame any rehabbers who lay this pursuit aside because of the difficulties. I haven't reached the seven-year mark quite yet. I'm just coming through my fifth season as I write this, so I can't be sure that I won't be among them.

Think about it: One of the largest, most successful rehab centers in the country, with the most knowledgeable staff and a wealth of great volunteers, can cite a successful live animal release rate of only a little under 50 percent. That means just over half of the animals that come in are unable to be released back to the wild, and a large percentage of those animals die of injury or illness. If more than half of whatever you were involved with day in and day out did not go very well (or went very poorly), you might feel like quitting too.

I won't spend a long time talking about the difficulties involved with wildlife rehab, but it's important to realize that some days are more challenging than others...

0 for 1, 0 for 2, 0 for 3...

"Hey, how's the wildlife thing going?" a well-meaning friend asks me one spring.

"Not so great yet," I reply. "I got in a cute little squirrel, but it must have taken a major fall. It couldn't move well and kept having seizures. All of the rehabbers I talked to for advice said it sounded like a neurological injury. They thought the squirrel might just need recovery time, but it got worse and worse instead of better. I'm starting off the season 0 for 1."

"Hey, are you rehabbing any animals right now?" another interested friend asks.

"Well, I had a cute little squirrel with a neurological injury, but it didn't make it. Then I took in a cat-bit bunny, and I treated its injuries and put it on antibiotics, hoping it would pull through. But it just couldn't make it and died of infection. Now I'm 0 for 2."

"Hey, what's happening in the Lion's Den?" another person inquires.

"First, this squirrel with seizures died. Then I got a cute little cat-bit bunny, but it died too. After that, four pinkie opossums came in, so young that their mouths were still tightly sealed except for the pinhole at the front (a weird thing with baby opossums). I tried to do something for them, but they were so little and so dehydrated that they died before I could get them to an opossum expert a couple of hours away. Now I'm 0 for 3, 0 for 4, 0 for 5, 0 for 6, all in one night."

"Hey, what's going on with your rehabbing these days?" asks the next person.

"Don't ask! I'll let you know when something comes in that actually lives for me to tell about..."

As a rehabber, when you make out your annual report of every animal you took in and what happened to each, the release statistics can sometimes be hard to look at. In irrefutable black-and-white, the required paperwork reminds you that at least half of the time you were working with animals too compromised to make it. Those creatures came to a less than desirable end, and you had to watch it happen.

The success cases that do thrive and survive are so exciting they make the disasters worth dealing with, but there's no doubt about it—losing animals is a gut-wrenching part of rehabbing. It takes some mental and emotional stamina to downplay the traumas and focus on the joys. I find I need to make a concerted effort to "Philippians 4:6 it," as a preacher I once heard put it. You may be familiar with the verse: "Do not be anxious about anything, but in every situation, by prayer and petition, with thanksgiving, present your requests to God" (NIV). When I do that in the discouraging times, I find that "the peace of God, which transcends all understanding" (verse 7) guards my heart and mind along the way.

It also helps to keep reading in that same Bible passage: "Whatever is true, whatever is noble, whatever is right, whatever is pure, whatever is lovely, whatever is admirable—if anything is excellent or praiseworthy—think about such things" (verse 8). When I put that into practice and think about how specially God has designed the animals and how He takes delight in them—even watching over a single sparrow that falls to the ground—it renews my courage, calmness, and conviction that I'm doing some good in spite of the difficult days.

Zoonosis Psychosis

Then there's the difficulty of disease. The term *zoonosis psychosis* itself sounds like a dread disease, doesn't it? Exactly. Merriam-Webster's dictionary defines a *zoonosis* (pronounced *zoh-uh-noh-sis*) as "a disease communicable from animals to man under natural conditions."[1] Webster also defines *psychosis* as "extreme mental unrest of an individual

---

[1] *Merriam-Webster Unabridged*, s.v. "Zoonosis," http://unabridged.merriam-webster.com/unabridged/zoonosis.

or of a social group especially in regard to situational factors of grave import."[2]

"Extreme mental unrest?" Exactly. "Grave import?" There's a play on words for rehabbers. People can pick up diseases from wildlife in certain cases that are grave enough to put them in the grave. That's definitely a downside of rehabbing! Precautions can be taken to prevent such tragedies; good hygiene alone provides much protection. Yet it becomes vitally important for rehabbers to know what zoonoses wild animals can carry and how those can be transmitted from their wild world to our civilized one. And I think sometimes with that knowledge comes the possibility of developing a human psychosis, never mind what the animals carry. Enter the maybe six-week-old raccoon kit that came my way a few seasons back from a local campground.

"Hello, I'm out at the campground, and there's a little raccoon here that's obviously an orphan. It has been pestering campers for days. Do you have room to take it in? It's so hungry!"

"Sure thing; I'll come take a look." I was still a relatively new rehabber at the time, working under a mentor, and I wasn't taking in sick or injured animals. But this raccoon kit looked neither. It was cute as a button. (Aren't all baby animals? Except pinkies.) And it seemed fine to me—till I got it back to the Lion's Den and it started displaying some weird and awful symptoms I was unfamiliar with. Disturbing thoughts run through my mind at moments like that—thoughts like *rabies*!

It wasn't rabies—not in a Michigan raccoon anyway. As I mentioned earlier, a confirmed case of a rabid raccoon has not occurred in Michigan in more than two decades, so we're still allowed to rehab that species. If and when an instance of rabies is verified in a raccoon or any other Michigan species, then rehabbers will no longer be able to take in that species—a safeguard to protect human health. Currently, such a prohibition is in force for bats and skunks here.

But because raccoons are still a rabies vector species (RVS) and it could happen, I would always rather be safe than sorry. I called a rehab

---

2   *Merriam-Webster Unabridged*, s.v. "Psychosis," http://unabridged.merriam-webster.com/unabridged/psychoses.

mentor right away. "Hey, this little raccoon I just picked up seemed fine at first, but it's going downhill fast. The way it's acting is making me mighty nervous!"

I described all its symptoms, and fortunately this mentor identified the problem as coccidiosis (a nasty disease all by itself).

"Come get the medicine I have on hand just for this illness," she told me, "and get some treatment going right away!"

That de-stressed me a little. Then she added, "Unfortunately, if the disease has taken too big a hold on too tiny an animal, we might not be able to get it under control in time. It sounds as if this baby was wandering around that campground for quite a while before they called you."

That re-stressed me a lot. I did all that she advised, yet the raccoon kit still died (stress off the charts). Suffice it to say that its final moments left Michael (who was holding the baby at the time) and me with some mental images I would rather not retain.

"I never, ever want to go through anything like that again," my husband said to me afterward. (Me neither.)

In addition to various illnesses, raccoons can carry parasites like *Baylisascaris procyonis*, or raccoon roundworm, which can also be fatal to humans. And raccoons can carry both canine and feline distemper, often fatal to pets. All of which prompts me to ask myself for the hundredth time, *Why are raccoons my favorite again?*

That's just for starters, in a single wildlife species. And it's also just the internal parasites and problems, not counting the external parasites like fleas and ticks. I frequently find it necessary to apply flea-and-tick repellent to wildlife babies that have lost their mother but brought her parasite load with them to the Lion's Den. All of which tempts me to indulge in a little zoonosis psychosis. Or maybe a lot, depending on how often I remember to repeat Psalm 121:7 to myself: "The Lord keeps you from all harm and watches over your life."

Not that I am presumptuous about that! I've studied which diseases are transmissible, how they are transmitted, and what kind of hygienic protocols to follow to keep them from transmitting themselves to my household or me. Long before the COVID-19 pandemic surfaced, I was already imagining particles of contagion on every surface I touched after handling wildlife, and I was already wearing personal protective equipment (PPE) and washing my hands continually. I had already developed the habit of being scrupulous about hygiene every single day, and sometimes I'm even a little nutty about it.

All Creation Groans

Every animal belongs to God, including the ill or injured ones. That's a perplexing thought, I know. But just as God knows every sparrow that falls to the ground, He knows the health status of every one of His other creatures. We simply live in a world where the fullness of His kingdom is both "now and not yet," as some of my favorite Bible teachers put it. Because of that, the line from the Lord's Prayer where we ask that the Father's will be done "on earth as it is in heaven" is still as vital for us to pray as when Jesus first instructed His disciples to do so.

I don't believe God's will is sickness and disease for us or for His creatures, yet those harsh realities are still part of this earthen realm we occupy until Christ comes again. While we wait for Jesus to return and restore this fallen world, all creation is indeed groaning toward that day. Romans 8:22 (NKJV) says that "the whole creation groans and labors." Part of the pain is that people, animals, and plants suffer sickness, death, and decay. Sometimes illnesses are healed—sometimes not. But always in God's larger view, there is hope for the future:

> What we suffer now is nothing compared to the glory he will give us later. For all creation is waiting patiently and hopefully for that future day when God will resurrect his children. For on that day thorns and thistles, sin, death, and decay—the things that overcame the world against its will at God's command—will all disappear, and the world around us will share in the glorious freedom from sin which God's children enjoy.
>
> For we know that even the things of nature, like animals and plants, suffer in sickness and death as they await this great event. And even we Christians, although we have the Holy Spirit within us as a foretaste of future glory, also

groan to be released from pain and suffering. We, too, wait anxiously for that day when God will give us our full rights as his children, including the new bodies he has promised us—bodies that will never be sick again and will never die (Romans 8:18-23 TLB).

The intricacies of if/when/why/how healings take place are in the hands of God and are outside our domain. What is in our hands to do is help those who are ill in any way we can, be it through prayer, practical assistance, or appropriate medical treatment. We likewise groan with all creation toward the day that Revelation 21:3-4 describes for us—a day yet to come after His return:

> Look, God's home is now among his people! He will live with them, and they will be his people. God himself will be with them. He will wipe every tear from their eyes, and there will be no more death or sorrow or crying or pain. All these things are gone forever.

Now, that's a day I certainly long for!

The Ultimate Difficulty

All kinds of things can take out a wild rehab animal in the blink of an eye—before I have time to do much of anything about it. Yet those deaths, believe it or not, are the "easier" ones to deal with. Or at least they are a little more guilt free than the very difficult ones that involve euthanasia. Making the decision to euthanize an animal is different from having a sick or injured creature come into rehab and soon die anyway in my care.

The animal that lingers—too ill or too injured to be brought back to health but still a day or so away from dying—is the hardest difficulty of all to face. At least in my state, rehabbers are allowed to make the determination to put such wild creatures out of their misery via humane euthanasia. No matter how quickly and painlessly it is carried out, euthanasia is unpleasant and awful. Still, there are times that rehabbers are thankful to have the option.

"Hello, I have a huge opossum that has been lying in the snow next to my house for several hours," a caller said. "I have no idea why it isn't moving, but it's definitely alive and suffering. What should I do? I'm nervous about approaching it too closely, and I can't drive."

"Let me come over and take a look," I answered and then headed the caller's way. The opossum was still alive when I got there, but it couldn't do more than lift itself up just a little and drag itself a few inches. No injuries were immediately apparent. Opossums here don't carry much disease either, but something was terribly wrong.

"I'll take it back to the Lion's Den," I told the finder. "Opossums really aren't meant for Michigan winters, yet here they are in droves, and they don't hibernate. They can suffer severe frostbite and get so hungry and weak that they can't function. When they're feeling like that, it's not unusual for them to position themselves next to the foundation of a house, which can provide a little of the warmth they crave. This opossum might just need a night or two in a quiet place with nourishment and heat. I'm going to settle it into a warm, dark cage with food and water and observe it for 24 hours. If there's no improvement, then something else is wrong. Do you have a shovel? Let's scoop this critter into the animal carrier I brought, and I'll take it with me and see what I can do for it."

"Great!" the finder said. "I can't stand watching it suffer lying out in the cold any longer. Let me know what happens with it."

Back at the Lion's Den, I offered the unhappy creature water, sardines, and carrots, which should have tempted any hungry opossum. It was breathing heavily, and it barely had the energy to react to my presence, never mind take any interest in my food offerings. I left it in a warm, dark, quiet cage overnight, but in the morning there was no improvement. Not one iota. So I made the difficult decision to transport it to a local animal shelter, where a worker euthanized it immediately.

Examining the poor animal with me afterward, this medically savvy shelter worker determined that it probably had an injured or possibly a punctured lung, which had likely resulted in pneumonia. A couple of what looked like older bite marks on its chest had been impossible to see without closer examination.

"I don't think there was anything you could have done to save this opossum in its present condition," the worker said. "It was too far gone. But at least we gently put it out of its misery, so that's something."

"It was so huge!" I said. "I imagine it must have had a very long, eventful life before whatever catastrophe befell it. For that much, I'm glad!"

Suffice it to say that euthanasia is a necessary evil that can sometimes be a kindness. It's one more example of the "kingdom both now and not yet" we face in this still imperfect world of ours.

I'm glad, too, that sometimes seemingly impossible cases do turn around unexpectedly and have a far happier ending than I could ever have envisioned at the start. Frodo, whose tale is next, is one of those cases. Tales like his offset the difficult days by many a mile.

14

A SINGLE RINGTAIL TALE

When he calls to me, I will answer him; I will be
with him in trouble; I will rescue him.

PSALM 91:15 ESV

A lot of good-hearted folks just cannot pass up an animal in distress, which I think is admirable. Somewhere inside each of us, we have a God-ordained inner drive to steward our Creator's creation, just as He assigned Adam and Eve to do. I believe God built that kind of concern and compassion into the very fiber of our being.

But at times, the best intentions can result in unintended outcomes (hi, George). People can find themselves in all kinds of unexpected or potentially harmful situations as an animal they've taken under their wing grows up and starts acting, well, like an animal. While these animals may indeed have needed to be rescued at the start, now the people involved may also need to be rescued.

Rescuing the Rescuers

Enter Frodo the raccoon. By the time I heard from his rescuers, they were in terrible trouble with him, and it was almost too late altogether for Frodo.

"Hello, we picked up this tiny, terrified raccoon baby next to its dead mother on the side of a busy road. We were afraid it would be hit by a car. We bottle-fed it and it's doing okay, but we've decided we can't keep it."

"Okay, I'm glad you rescued it! But what kind of formula are you using? If it's not the right kind, it can make the baby sick."

"Oh, Frodo isn't on formula anymore. He's weaned, so he eats almost anything."

"How long have you had this baby?" I asked.

"Oh, it's been a few months," they answered. "We've been keeping Frodo caged out in our shed. We wanted to keep him as a pet because we knew someone who used to have a pet raccoon that was really fun. But then we got busy and didn't have time to handle him much, and now he'll be way too hard to tame. Can you take him?"

Naming this kit after a favorite fictional character, Frodo from The Lord of the Rings, these rescuers managed to keep him alive via bottle-feeding—no small feat as by now I'm sure you've noticed that much of what people feed to wild babies kills them. But then these rescuers' kindness turned unintentionally unkind when they confined this tiny critter all by himself, day and night, in a cage in their shed. For months, Frodo had no sibling playmates, no mother's warmth and training, no exposure to the big outdoors, and very little human contact. That last part wasn't a bad thing; wariness of humans would be a good thing if he could ever be released into the wild. But the rest of it added up to a really rough patch for the little guy.

I say *if* he could ever be released because, although his rescuers had saved Frodo from physical harm on the roadside, I was pretty sure that they had inadvertently harmed his mind or instincts or whatever you prefer to call a little animal's "thinking" processes. The way they had isolated Frodo at that early developmental stage of his life must have been sheer misery for him. As you might expect, he soon grew unhappy and unmanageable under those circumstances.

At the point that these now-desperate people had decided some kind of change was needed for Frodo, three choices were left for him, two of which would be fatal. One, he could be euthanized to put him (and them) out of his misery. The rescuers told me they considered that option but couldn't bear to think about it, having grown attached to their "pet" raccoon (or at least to the idea of it).

Two, they could simply open up his crate somewhere in the woods and let him go themselves, which thankfully they realized would be a death sentence for him. The odds of this lone raccoon kit surviving his first winter in the wild—with no others of his kind and no experience feeding himself, finding shelter, or avoiding predators—were almost certainly zero.

Three, they could put him in the hands of a wildlife rehabilitator and hope for the best. That's the option they chose, so that's where I came into the story. Frodo needed a new lease on life, if such a thing was possible.

If only these finders had turned the tiny raccoon over to a rehabber right when they found him! At best, he would have been introduced to other orphans the same size, and he could have grown up gleefully wrestling around with his playmates. Raccoon kits *need* to play rough! At worst, as a single he would have been raised with plenty of warmth and affection from a human rehab "parent," which tiny single raccoons need, while the search would have been on among rehabber networks to place him with others of his own kind. Instead, this sorry little raccoon had sat enclosed alone in a cage, shoved away in a shed, during the most vital stage of his development. Nothing good ever comes of that approach.

I didn't read these people the riot act when they called, although some rehabbers certainly would have. But nothing good ever comes of that, either. So instead of expressing my horror at what they had done to Frodo, I consoled myself with the thought that at least they had rescued him from his initial danger and were choosing to do the right thing by him in the end. Hoping for better things ahead for this poor guy, I simply told them, "Yes, of course I'll take him."

Long, Uncertain Odds

What I observed when they brought Frodo to the Lion's Den wasn't pretty. Physically, he was magnificent. Obviously, they had never neglected to feed him. He was the picture of health on the outside, with a plump belly and a luxurious coat of fur.

His stress level on the inside, however, was painfully apparent. His aggressive behavior as they carried his wire crate from the car to my wildlife shed had me taking a step back. Not literally; I did all I could to make sure his transfer from crate to rehab cage went safely for him—and more importantly, for us. Yet his arrival was not a peace-filled moment. I made a mental note to keep my hands and fingers well out of Frodo's reach at all times.

I imagine he was frustrated at being confined for so long in an isolated, unstimulating atmosphere. Added to that, he must have been completely terrified by the trip from their place to mine. The way he curled into a sorry-looking ball in the bottom corner of the rehab cage made me want to cry.

Taking Our Best Shot

Standing next to Frodo (and out of reach) after the drop-off, I waved good-bye to his finders and did indeed cry a few tears at the pathetic sight of him. Then it was time to dry my tears and take action. I talked over his case with a raccoon-savvy rehab mentor and put a plan in place. First, Frodo would spend a few nights in the wildlife shed so I could observe him and check his overall health. Second, I would worm him for the insidious raccoon roundworms, which the rescuers had never done (horror of horrors). Third, I would make sure he was eating well. Based on the look of him, he had a hefty appetite. Eating was probably the only thing he had ever had a chance to enjoy.

The rehab cage was much larger than anything Frodo was used to, so I didn't feel too terrible about keeping him confined in the Lion's Den for a few days. And there was a hammock hanging up in the top for him, should he choose to use it. Every raccoon I have ever known has been positively fanatical about hanging around in hammocks. They love to be up high, looking down on the world. Frodo had never had the opportunity to climb, much less hang out on high, so I tossed some nice treats into the hammock and watched to see if the sorry little ball of fur at the bottom of the cage would uncurl itself.

Nothing happened. Frodo stayed stock-still, other than tipping his head a little to glare at me with one eye. Figuring he was stressed by the move and the change of scenery, I stepped out of the shed and gave him some privacy. When I stepped back in a little later, two bright eyes stared out at me from the hammock, and the treats were gone. He looked wary at my approach and made a few threatening noises, but unless I was imagining it, he also looked a little bit pleased with himself. While he watched me closely from "upstairs," I put on some hefty gloves and quickly took the opportunity to make sure he had adequate food and water "downstairs" in his cage. Then we said goodnight (or one of us did, anyway).

The next day, Frodo glued himself into the hammock unless he needed food or water. He slept away that whole first day, probably exhausted from having his whole life as he knew it turned upside down. He became much more active the day after that, although no less wary. He was healthy, all right, which I was glad to see. And I had managed to make sure that he took in some worming medicine along with his much-loved food. That meant we were ready to take the next step in my plan and move him out to the raccoon release cage in the woods.

Except that I would need to get him into a plastic pet carrier to move him. No way was I going to use my hands for that! When he was upstairs in his hammock, I speedily put the pet carrier into the bottom corner of the cage, filling it with treats at the back and leaving its door propped wide open. I left it there for 24 hours, throwing treats into it at every opportunity. It didn't take long for him to get quite used to going inside the carrier face first to eat.

As soon as we reached that point, I readied the big release cage by the pond. Conveniently, no other raccoons were residing in it at the time. Given to me by a rehabber friend, that cage is a Raccoon Hilton. It's several times the size of the raccoon cage in the wildlife shed, with a really high, really big hammock. It also sports logs to climb up, a high ledge to zip around on, and sturdy wire that allows for a panoramic view of the surrounding wilderness. Raccoon Hilton would be by far the biggest place in which Frodo had ever stretched his legs.

Once the release cage was ready, I placed another pile of alluring snacks at the back of the pet carrier in his current cage. The instant Frodo dove inside to eat them, I reached my hand in the cage faster than the speed of light and fastened the carrier door shut behind him. Naturally, that dastardly act on my part greatly displeased him, but

I had gotten used to his baleful glare by then. I knew his discomfort would last only a few minutes, and then he would be in for the time of his life.

Frodo was no lightweight! I popped the raccoon-heavy carrier into our wheelbarrow, still mindful of keeping my hands well protected. Just how much a hefty junior raccoon can weigh is mind-boggling. When nicely plump, they often look like bowling balls, albeit with legs and a tail, and they weigh about the same. Then I wheeled him out into the woods. Transferring the carrier into the Raccoon Hilton, I sprung the latch on its door. Again with the speed of light, I pulled my hand away and fastened the outer release cage door tightly so he would be securely confined.

Frodo shows a new interest in life

Frodo didn't stay stock-still this time. More used to my presence, he ignored me and explored the Hilton with glee—up and down the logs, around and around the high ledge, up and across the huge hammock. For once in his life he seemed energized and enthused, and it thrilled me to the core to watch that transformation.

It All Depends...

I left Frodo to it, hoping that what the rehab mentor and I had in mind was going to work. Success wouldn't depend on him alone. It would also depend on some other young raccoons I had recently released in the same spot. If they would induct Frodo as a member of their gang, it would astronomically improve his chances of going over to the wild side. So the next part of our plan was to install the woods camera and watch what happened on the outside of the cage with them, as well as on the inside of the cage with him.

Typically, the thing to do with a singleton raccoon is to network with other rehabbers to find other raccoons that can serve as its adopted siblings. This just wasn't possible to do for Frodo. He qualified as a rare exception because of the timing, his attitude and age, and the release limitations in our area, all of which were working against him. As I've mentioned, my state's disease containment rules say raccoons must be released in the county in which they are born. That meant I couldn't have taken him very far to join other raccoons anyway.

At worst, my rehab mentor and I figured Frodo could continue living in the release cage after I opened the door, coming and going as he pleased. I would supplement feed him long-term, and he could enjoy a little taste of freedom in the woods at our place for as long as he managed to survive.

In this shot from my woods camera,
Frodo is starting to explore the nighttime woods

At best, we were hoping for a far better outcome. Raccoons sometimes lead solitary lives, but other times, especially if they are young or food is plentiful, they'll hang around together in a big group. I had never released more than three or four raccoons at a time by the pond, but the woods camera frequently showed groups of eight or more eating together. We had high hopes that Frodo would soon become an accepted member of such a gang—if the other rehabbed raccoons running around back there would play nice.

To my delight, the resident raccoon gang didn't fail to deliver! Two raccoons of similar size to Frodo started showing up in late-night cameo shots outside his cage. Inside and out, they all seemed to show great interest in one another, and the two wildish ones made repeat appearances on subsequent evenings.

"Open the door!" my mentor exclaimed when I told her what I was seeing take place on camera between the raccoons. "Let's let him go and see what happens."

One of the Gang

When I opened the door to the wild world for Frodo, I didn't stand around to watch his reaction. I wanted to give him the space to explore the woods for the first time, unimpeded by my human presence. (Admittedly, I also wanted to stay out of his reach.) Once I offered him his freedom, he was quick to take advantage of it. I carefully checked the cage after a few hours and saw no sign of him. Yet from the telltale signs I did see over the next few days, he seemed to make the transition into the wild very quickly, aided by his already rehabbed raccoon cohorts. His rough start in life did not turn out to be a life sentence— or worse, a death sentence—after all.

I have continued to keep one eye on Frodo with the woods camera, and I even ran into him not long after his release. He was hanging out in a tree near Raccoon Hilton with those two wilder raccoons, apparently as one of the gang—a very good development. How did I know it was the same guy? Of the three raccoons I ran into that day, the other two shot high up in the tree right away and hid on the far side, doing their best to stay well out of sight. (As they should do in the presence of a human.) The recently released Frodo did not. He went a little way up the tree, following the others (also a good development), but then he stopped on a branch not far above my head and turned around to stare at me with those bright, no longer baleful eyes. Obviously, he had a question for me: "What's for dinner?" (Again, Momma didn't raise— or at least in this case briefly take care of—no dummy. I did indeed have a pail of supplement feed in my hand.)

By all indications ever since, Frodo no longer lives in the open release cage, although he continues to be fond of the supplement feed, which disappears at regular intervals. Now that he has joined the rest of the resident raccoon gang, I imagine he has a little help making that happen. Beyond those secondhand signs of his presence, it looks as though Frodo is well and truly living on the wild side, back where he belongs. And he's not alone. It's no longer a single ringtail tale.

15

BECAUSE HE CARES, WE CARE

*Whatever you do, in word or deed, do everything in the name of
the Lord Jesus, giving thanks to God the Father through him.*

Colossians 3:17 esv

Reliving some of my favorite wildlife adventures brings a favorite poem to mind. Most people are familiar with its first stanza, which James Herriot popularized in his book series about his veterinarian practice in the Yorkshire Dales. The original author of the poem, however, was Anglican hymn lyricist Cecil Frances Alexander, who first wrote these lines in her 1848 version of *Hymns for Little Children*. Very appropriately, then, they actually form the first verse of a famous hymn of praise to God:

> All things bright and beautiful,
> All creatures great and small,
> All things wise and wonderful,
> The Lord God made them all.

The second verse of the hymn is lovely, too, especially the "tiny wings" part:

> Each little flower that opens,
> Each little bird that sings,
> He made their glowing colours,
> He made their tiny wings.

I won't reproduce the whole hymn, but my favorite is the seventh and last verse, which goes,

> He gave us eyes to see them,
> And lips that we might tell,
> How great is God Almighty,
> Who has made all things well.

We just cannot escape the fact that God cares deeply about everything He made. And because He cares, we care. As believers, we can have God's heart for humankind and also have His heart for His other creatures. I believe He gave us big enough hearts that there is room for both.

I realize that humankind is unique. God literally breathed His very breath of life into us: "Then the LORD God formed the man from the dust of the ground. He breathed the breath of life into the man's nostrils, and the man became a living person" (Genesis 2:7). In the Hebrew, that "breath" of life, or *nĕshamah*, can be translated as "spirit."[1] We are spirit, as God is Spirit. In that way, we humans are uniquely a reflection of Him, and we are therefore capable of relating to Him in a unique way. That is the priceless privilege of our kind. Yet the particular delight He takes in us in no way negates the delight He takes in the rest of this earth's creatures.

Not to Mention All the Animals...

For all the intrinsic value God places on His human children, I think His Word indicates that He also places a great deal of value on the animals. It tickles me every time I read through God's conversation with Jonah outside the city of Nineveh. Certainly, He sent Jonah to that sin-wracked city to preach repentance to the many thousands of lost human souls, that they might avoid the destruction their sin threatened them with and get things right with God. But notice God's parting comment to Jonah in the very last verse of the Bible book that bears Jonah's name: "Nineveh has more than 120,000 people living in

---

[1] *Blue Letter Bible* Lexicon online, Strong's H5397, s.v. *nĕshamah*, www.blueletterbible.org/lang/lexicon/lexicon.cfm?Strongs=H5397.

spiritual darkness, *not to mention all the animals*. Shouldn't I feel sorry for such a great city?" (Jonah 4:11, emphasis added).

Imagine God dropping in that comment about His creatures right at the end as a parting thought: *not to mention all the animals*. Our Creator was reluctant to see the city of Nineveh destroyed, and this was primarily because of—but not *only* because of—His human children toward whom His compassion flowed. God was also concerned because of *all the animals*. That shouts to me of their importance. While animals may not be the pinnacle of His creation, His compassion flows toward them in some measure, just as it flows toward us.

If animals were of little or no value to God, He would have had no reason to mention them to Jonah or to see that His comment was recorded in Scripture for us to read throughout the ages. And that does not even take into account the book of Jonah's mention of that famous or infamous "whale" (if indeed that's what this big sea creature was—a point scholars are still debating). What Sunday school child can forget hearing for the first time the story of Jonah spending three days and nights in the belly of a big fish? I have to believe that it tickled God to orchestrate such a phenomenal event using one of His most magnificent creatures of the sea. In fact, have you ever read this glorious description of the sea creatures?

> Here is the ocean, vast and wide,
>   teeming with life of every kind,
>   both large and small.
> See the ships sailing along,
>   and Leviathan, which you made to play in the sea.
>
> They all depend on you
>   to give them food as they need it.
> When you supply it, they gather it.
>   You open your hand to feed them,
>   and they are richly satisfied (Psalm 104:25-28).

This Scripture says that the ocean, vast and wide, is teeming with all kinds of life, large and small. What enchanting images—an ocean literally swimming with life and a God who opens His hand and satisfies the needs of every living thing.

Apparently God enjoys, cares for, and is even amused by the wealth of creatures that He made in addition to humankind. Of course, I want to love and care about *people*, as He does. Yet the fact that He would have compassion on the animals gives me reason enough to have compassion on them as well. I want God's character and love to shine through my compassionate heart toward all His creatures. He took great care intricately designing the birds and beasts, and then He took great care putting humankind in charge of stewarding them. That charge to steward them plays out in my life through my wildlife rehabilitation. It may play out in other ways in your life. But for all of us, I think it is meant to play out somehow.

Doing What I Do...

I certainly don't expect everyone to do what I do with wildlife. Your journey walking with the Lord will not look the same as mine or anyone else's. Together we form one body of Christ, but with many different parts and just as many individual gifts (see Romans 12:4-6; 1 Corinthians 12:12-31). If you and I each do the things God tells us to do in this area and others, everything He wants us to accomplish will get done!

Having acknowledged that, I want to mention that if you are drawn to doing wildlife rehabilitation, you'll want to do your homework first and make sure it's a good fit for you.[2] Each country and even each state in the United States has its own requirements for wildlife rehabbing, often including putting in some class time and volunteer hours and then taking a test. Usually, an online search about wildlife rehabilitation in your area will bring up a wealth of information.[3]

---

[2] One helpful tool in analyzing whether or not wildlife rehab is a good fit is Peggy Hentz's four-part YouTube series "Introduction to Wildlife Rehabilitation," in which she details the ins and outs and ups and downs of this activity. You can find part 1 at https://www.youtube.com/watch?v=l9NY74uanm8.

[3] Another helpful tool that would be informative for anyone is the article "Wildlife Rehabilitation: Is It for You?" on Michigan's Department of Natural Resources website: https://www.michigan.gov/documents/dnr/WLD_Wildlife_Rehabilitation-Is_It_For_You_341551_7.pdf. By googling the article title, you'll find many similar articles from different states and organizations.

In addition, you can visit my website, trishann.com, to see more stories and pictures about what day-to-day wildlife rehabilitation can involve. Everywhere I know, rehabbers are in high demand and short supply. Your involvement would be welcome!

Stories Yet to Unfold

Along our way in these pages, I have shared some stories about the most memorable wild creatures that have come and gone under my care (with the exception of Pigeon George, who never would go anywhere else). Skeeter and that first Ringtail Gang were unrivaled at turning our lives upside down. That first bunch of ringtails was a huge challenge and no mistake, although I made plenty of mistakes with them on my steep learning curve.

Spark's transformation—from a little pinkie ember baking away in a hot parking lot to a flaming red squirrel racing up and down trees, wild and free—was an unrivaled joy to see.

Pigeon George became the poster pigeon for wildlife rehab gone wrong—the unrivaled expert at teaching me how wildlife rehab can go sideways, into the unexpected.

Jay-Jay and the Early Birds demonstrated how fiercely determined or achingly fragile the feathered species can be. The birds of the air are the winged wonders of creation, no mistake.

Bunny the sole survivor and Frodo the singleton ringtail proved how much hope there is for the hopeless. Frodo's story also showed that even the rescuers sometimes need rescuing, and there's hope for that too. I was thrilled to play a part in those success stories.

I'm confident that many more wildlife tales are yet to unfold and are yet to be told, and each story will be unique and amazing. As I write this, spring season is creeping up on us in Northern Michigan. Warmer weather is only a month or so away, although it can be hard to pinpoint its arrival in the Mitten State. Whenever spring arrives, rehabbers everywhere will become wildly busy again after their winter break, and the Lion's Den will begin to fill up again. And I'll marvel all over again at the wonder of the creatures great and small, and the way that their Creator loves them all.

FAVORITE ANIMAL VERSES

All Scripture is God-breathed and is useful for teaching, rebuking,
correcting and training in righteousness, so that the servant
of God may be thoroughly equipped for every good work.

2 Timothy 3:16-17 niv

For a long time I have kept a list of my favorite Bible verses that relate in some way to animals. Whenever I run across such a verse, I jot it down on a slip of paper or a napkin or a gum wrapper and toss it into a little basket I've set aside to collect them. Now and again I pull out all these little scraps and read through the animal verses just for the joy of it, which serves to keep my wonder at the magnificence of God's creativity fresh. It never ceases to delight and amaze me that He includes in His Word so many references to the animal world I love.

As a finishing touch, I want to share my favorite animal verses with you. Note that what you'll see here is by no means an exhaustive list of Scriptures that mention animals. This is simply a list of those animal verses that have jumped out at me, as passages quickened for us by the Holy Spirit are wont to do. These particular passages in the Bible have gripped my heart because of my wont to focus on the furred and feathered creatures with which we share this earth.

If you are an animal lover, you may have other favorite verses of your own that you would include here. By all means, add them in the margins if you wish. Note that throughout, I have added my comments in *italics* following some of the passages, in which I explain either why they stood out to me or what I think they might signify. Note also that these Scriptures are taken from a variety of Bible translations since each translation has its own unique flavor.

Old Testament Animal Verses

Genesis 1:24-25

God said, "Let the earth produce every sort of animal, each producing offspring of the same kind—livestock, small animals that scurry along the ground, and wild animals." And that is what happened. God made all sorts of wild animals, livestock, and small animals, each able to produce offspring of the same kind. And God saw that it was good.

Genesis 1:27-28 ESV

God created man in his own image, in the image of God he created him; male and female he created them. And God blessed them. And God said to them, "Be fruitful and multiply and fill the earth and subdue it, and have dominion over the fish of the sea and over the birds of the heavens and over every living thing that moves on the earth."

Genesis 2:19-20 NIV

Now the LORD God had formed out of the ground all the wild animals and all the birds in the sky. He brought them to the man to see what he would name them; and whatever the man called each living creature, that was its name. So the man gave names to all the livestock, the birds in the sky and all the wild animals.

When reading these verses, I have often told God that naming the animals is one job I would have liked—although facing the serpent in the Garden does not sound equally appealing. I hope that in eternity, we get to see a video replay of this scene between Adam and the animals.

Genesis 7:7-9 NKJV

Noah, with his sons, his wife, and his sons' wives, went into the ark because of the waters of the flood. Of clean animals, of animals that are unclean, of birds, and of everything that creeps on the earth, two by two they went into the ark to Noah, male and female, as God had commanded Noah.

This is another passage where reading it has me telling God how much I would have liked that job—or maybe not Noah's huge task, since I'm not that great at building boats and am terrible at working with sharp tools. But at least his wife's job of helping care for all those creatures on the Ark— that is something I think I would have done gladly. I hope this scene between Noah and the animals is the second half of a double feature in eternity, combined with the video replay of the scene just mentioned in Genesis 2.

Exodus 12:31-32 NIV

During the night Pharaoh summoned Moses and Aaron and said, "Up! Leave my people, you and the Israelites! Go, worship the LORD as you have requested. Take your flocks and herds, as you have said, and go. And also bless me."

When the Israelites left Egypt during the Exodus, they took their flocks and herds with them. I would have wanted to do the same. I'm attached to my chickens.

Exodus 20:8-10

Remember to observe the Sabbath day by keeping it holy. You have six days each week for your ordinary work, but the seventh day is a Sabbath day of rest dedicated to the LORD your God. On that day no one in your household may do any work. This includes you, your sons and daughters, your male and female servants, your livestock, and any foreigners living among you.

Note that the Lord commands rest not only for His people, but also for their livestock. He gives the animals a day of rest too!

Numbers 22:22-23, 28 HCSB

God was incensed that Balaam was going, and the Angel of the LORD took His stand on the path to oppose him. Balaam was riding his donkey, and his two servants were with him. When the donkey saw the Angel of the LORD standing on the path with a drawn sword in His hand, she turned off the path and went into the field. So Balaam hit her to return her to the path... Then the LORD opened the donkey's mouth, and she asked Balaam, "What have I done to you that you have beaten me these three times?"

This whole passage is a hilarious tale in which the donkey sees an angel

and tries to give way, while her human master, Balaam, is completely insen-
sitive spiritually. God even has the donkey talk to her master—a "one time
only in the course of human events" happening, as far as we know. God also
opens Balaam's eyes to see the angel eventually, but in this story the donkey
definitely comes across as the smart one.

Deuteronomy 28:8 NIV

The LORD will send a blessing on your barns and on everything
you put your hand to. The LORD your God will bless you in the land
he is giving you.

This is a good verse that I like to reference while praying health and
healing over any livestock or other creatures in my care.

I Kings 4:33-34

He [Solomon] could speak with authority about all kinds of plants,
from the great cedar of Lebanon to the tiny hyssop that grows from
cracks in a wall. He could also speak about animals, birds, small creatures, and fish. And kings from every nation sent their ambassadors to
listen to the wisdom of Solomon.

Part of King Solomon's reputation for greatness was that he owned a
vast number of animals, and part of his reputation for wisdom had to do
with his vast knowledge of the animal kingdom. Some translations even
say that he taught about them. I wish I were that wise about animals. I'm
working on it!

Job 12:7-10 NIV

But ask the animals, and they will teach you, or the birds in the sky,
and they will tell you; or speak to the earth, and it will teach you, or let
the fish in the sea inform you. Which of all these does not know that
the hand of the LORD has done this? In his hand is the life of every creature and the breath of all mankind.

If we as humans don't recognize the greatness of God, we are falling
behind the rest of His creation.

Psalm 36:6-7

You care for people and animals alike, O LORD. How precious is your unfailing love, O God! All humanity finds shelter in the shadow of your wings.

Psalm 50:10-11

All the animals of the forest are mine [says the Lord], and I own the cattle on a thousand hills. I know every bird on the mountains, and all the animals of the field are mine.

This is my "theme" passage at the Lion's Den. I think God's inclusiveness here of all His creatures is so powerful and lovely. The original Hebrew wording indicates that He is including everything from insects to field mice to wild beasts when He says all the animals of the field are His.

Psalm 55:6-7

Oh, that I had wings like a dove; then I would fly away and rest! I would fly far away to the quiet of the wilderness.

Like the writer of this psalm, many people have found the quiet of the wilderness a holy place of solace.

Psalm 84:3 NIV

Even the sparrow has found a home, and the swallow a nest for herself, where she may have her young—a place near your altar, LORD Almighty, my King and my God.

I do think God's creatures are drawn to Him, even as the birds of the air were drawn near the altar of His Temple in this verse.

Psalm 104:10-12 HCSB

He causes the springs to gush into the valleys; they flow between the mountains. They supply water for every wild beast; the wild donkeys quench their thirst. The birds of the sky live beside the springs; they sing among the foliage.

God is and always has been the Source of water for everything on earth, not to mention being the Living Water for us.

Psalm 104:20-23 HCSB

You bring darkness, and it becomes night, when all the forest animals stir. The young lions roar for their prey and seek their food from God. The sun rises; they go back and lie down in their dens. Man goes out to his work and to his labor until evening.

Look at God's design for many predatory creatures to stir by night and for humans to stir by day in a sort of trade-off that often keeps them out of each other's way.

Psalm 104:24

O LORD, what a variety of things you have made! In wisdom you have made them all. The earth is full of your creatures.

Psalm 145:9

The LORD is good to everyone. He showers compassion on all his creation.

Psalm 145:16 NIV

You open your hand and satisfy the desires of every living thing.

Psalm 147:9

He gives food to the wild animals and feeds the young ravens when they cry.

Psalm 148:7-10 NIV

Praise the LORD from the earth, you great sea creatures and all ocean depths, lightning and hail, snow and clouds, stormy winds that do his bidding, you mountains and all hills, fruit trees and all cedars, wild animals and all cattle, small creatures and flying birds.

This passage, along with some verses like Psalm 150:6, intimates that in some way, on some level, even the animals and other created things are capable of praising their Creator. I find the mention of sea monsters in some translations amusing as well. Who knows the depth of all the created things living in those ocean depths? The Loch Ness monster may be, in some form or another, more than fable.

Psalm 150:6 ESV

Let everything that has breath praise the LORD!

Proverbs 12:10 NIV

The righteous care for the needs of their animals, but the kindest acts of the wicked are cruel.

I often send the first half of this verse to friends and relatives who are mourning the loss of a beloved pet, both to comfort them and to reassure them that the good care and life they gave their favorite creature was a form of righteousness in God's eyes.

Proverbs 27:23-24 HCSB

Know well the condition of your flock, and pay attention to your herds, for wealth is not forever; not even a crown lasts for all time.

This great passage talks about our stewardship in the economic realm. Flocks and herds were the currency of the day when it was written.

Isaiah 1:3

Even an ox knows its owner, and a donkey recognizes its master's care.

I like the way the Bible confirms here that the creatures in our care indeed know and recognize us in some way.

Isaiah 11:6-9

In that day the wolf and the lamb will live together; the leopard will lie down with the baby goat. The calf and the yearling will be safe with the lion, and a little child will lead them all. The cow will graze near the bear. The cub and the calf will lie down together. The lion will eat hay like a cow. The baby will play safely near the hole of a cobra. Yes, a little child will put its hand in a nest of deadly snakes without harm. Nothing will hurt or destroy in all my holy mountain, for as the waters fill the sea, so the earth will be filled with people who know the LORD.

I, for one, will be thrilled if Christ's return and the "new heavens and new earth" does a reboot of the wild kingdom, so that once again we enjoy the relationship with wildlife that Adam and Eve and their pre-Fall

/pre-Flood descendants must have enjoyed. Once the Flood came, everything about humankind's relationship with the animals changed (see Genesis 9:1-3). But hope of restoration is on its way with Christ's coming again.

Isaiah 43:20

The wild animals in the fields will thank me, the jackals and owls, too, for giving them water in the desert. Yes, I will make rivers in the dry wasteland so my chosen people can be refreshed.

Isaiah 65:25 NIV

"The wolf and the lamb will feed together, and the lion will eat straw like the ox, and dust will be the serpent's food. They will neither harm nor destroy on all my holy mountain," says the LORD.

Jeremiah 27:4-5

This is what the LORD of Heaven's Armies, the God of Israel, says: With my great strength and powerful arm I made the earth and all its people and every animal. I can give these things of mine to anyone I choose.

Here am I, Lord. You can give some animals to me!

Jeremiah 28:14

The LORD of Heaven's Armies, the God of Israel, says: I have put a yoke of iron on the necks of all these nations, forcing them into slavery under King Nebuchadnezzar of Babylon. I have put everything, even the wild animals, under his control.

This verse is interesting in that God can choose to put wild animals under a person's control, as perhaps was also the case with Noah and his family. I'd be up for that, although I'd be careful not to presume on it by taking careless risks around animals.

Hosea 2:18

On that day I will make a covenant with all the wild animals and the birds of the sky and the animals that scurry along the ground so they will not harm you.

Another verse I'd be up for, although again I would not be presumptuous.

Jonah 4:10-11

Then the LORD said, "...Nineveh has more than 120,000 people living in spiritual darkness, not to mention all the animals. Shouldn't I feel sorry for such a great city?"

Not to mention all the animals! Every time I read the way God mentions the animals to Jonah in this context, it strikes me all over again how much He cares about them too.

Habakkuk 2:17

You cut down the forests of Lebanon. Now you will be cut down. You destroyed the wild animals, so now their terror will be yours.

A striking verse in which God didn't seem happy at all about the wild animals being destroyed. I know it's said that you can't stand in the way of progress, but every time I pass a construction site, I wonder what the progress there meant for the wild animals once calling that patch of ground home.

Zechariah 14:20

On that day [of the Lord] even the harness bells of the horses will be inscribed with these words: HOLY TO THE LORD.

The presence of horses in eternity seems to be a recurring idea in Scripture; they are mentioned in Revelation, the final book of the New Testament, as well. No complaints here; count me in! There's a particular pony I'd like to have back when I get there...

New Testament Animal Verses

Matthew 6:26 NIV

Look at the birds of the air; they do not sow or reap or store away in barns, and yet your heavenly Father feeds them. Are you not much more valuable than they?

Matthew 10:29-31 NIV

Are not two sparrows sold for a penny? Yet not one of them will fall to the ground outside your Father's care. And even the very hairs of your head are all numbered. So don't be afraid; you are worth more than many sparrows.

This passage is reassuring, given the sheer number of sparrows that fall to the ground. Scientific estimates place the number of common house sparrows at 150 million in the United State alone, and they exist pretty much everywhere else in the world too. Yet for all the arguably billions of sparrows, the Father knows exactly what each one of them is up to in life and in death. If He keeps track of the sparrows that closely, then we can trust that He is keeping even closer track of us.

Matthew 21:1-7

As Jesus and the disciples approached Jerusalem, they came to the town of Bethphage on the Mount of Olives. Jesus sent two of them on ahead. "Go into the village over there," he said. "As soon as you enter it, you will see a donkey tied there, with its colt beside it. Untie them and bring them to me. If anyone asks what you are doing, just say, 'The Lord needs them,' and he will immediately let you take them."

This took place to fulfill the prophecy that said, "Tell the people of Jerusalem, 'Look, your King is coming to you. He is humble, riding on a donkey—riding on a donkey's colt.'"

The two disciples did as Jesus commanded. They brought the donkey and the colt to him and threw their garments over the colt, and he sat on it.

Notice that Jesus was aware of these animals and their whereabouts ahead of time, which makes me think He may have made arrangements with the owner long beforehand. I like the way He also made sure that the mother donkey was brought along with the colt, which had to be of great comfort to the young animal amidst the noisy crowd.

Mark 1:12-13 NIV

At once the Spirit sent him [Jesus after His baptism] out into the wilderness, and he was in the wilderness forty days, being tempted by Satan. He was with the wild animals, and angels attended him.

It fascinates me that wild animals get this special mention of being around Jesus during that trying 40 days of His life.

Mark 11:7-9 NKJV

Then they brought the colt to Jesus and threw their clothes on it, and He sat on it. And many spread their clothes on the road, and others cut down leafy branches from the trees and spread them on the road. Then those who went before and those who followed cried out, saying: "Hosanna! 'Blessed is He who comes in the name of the LORD!'"

This is another Bible book's mention of the time Jesus gets on the back of a colt that has never been ridden. As I said in chapter 1, surely to stay so calm, the colt must have recognized something about the One it was carrying!

Luke 2:4-7 ESV

Joseph also went up from Galilee, from the town of Nazareth, to Judea, to the city of David, which is called Bethlehem, because he was of the house and lineage of David, to be registered with Mary, his betrothed, who was with child. And while they were there, the time came for her to give birth. And she gave birth to her firstborn son and wrapped him in swaddling cloths and laid him in a manger, because there was no place for them in the inn.

Granted, the manger is the closest thing to an animal mentioned in this passage, but imagine how, from the first moment of His arrival on earth as a baby, Jesus was with the animals—or at least near them. The very Son of God was born in a stable, of all places! And tradition tells us, although Scripture does not, that Mary was riding on a donkey on her journey toward the Savior's birthplace anyway. Given the distance and how great she was with child, I think she must indeed have needed to ride, and what else could have eased her way more than to travel atop the back of a strong, warm, fuzzy friend?

Luke 14:3-6 NKJV

Jesus, answering, spoke to the lawyers and Pharisees, saying, "Is it lawful to heal on the Sabbath?"

But they kept silent. And He took him [a man with dropsy] and healed him, and let him go. Then He answered them, saying, "Which of you, having a donkey or an ox that has fallen into a pit, will not immediately pull him out on the Sabbath day?" And they could not answer Him regarding these things.

Jesus simply assumes we would know that an animal struggling in a pit is worth rescuing, even when it means an owner is breaking the Sabbath.

Luke 16:19-21

Jesus said, "There was a certain rich man who was splendidly clothed in purple and fine linen and who lived each day in luxury. At his gate lay a poor man named Lazarus who was covered with sores. As Lazarus lay there longing for scraps from the rich man's table, the dogs would come and lick his open sores."

If you're a dog owner, you know how your canine companions seem to sense when you are feeling unwell. I'm not sure whether these were street dogs or belonged to the rich man, but whatever the case, the dogs around the beggar Lazarus displayed the same kind of built-in radar and tried to comfort him in their own way.

John 1:29

Look! The Lamb of God who takes away the sin of the world!

Our Savior certainly is the sacrificial Lamb of God in my mind and heart, along with being the wild and victorious Lion of Judah.

John 10:27-30 ESV

My sheep hear my voice, and I know them, and they follow me. I give them eternal life, and they will never perish, and no one will snatch them out of my hand. My Father, who has given them to me, is greater than all, and no one is able to snatch them out of the Father's hand. I and the Father are one.

I have never had sheep, but I think they're enticing. All that fluffiness!

I don't mind being characterized as one of the Good Shepherd's sheep. I would not want to be a goat in the Matthew 25:31-46 passage, however, where He separates the "sheep" from the "goats" who don't make it into the kingdom!

Romans 8:19-22 HCSB

The creation eagerly waits with anticipation for God's sons to be revealed. For the creation was subjected to futility—not willingly, but because of Him who subjected it—in the hope that the creation itself will also be set free from the bondage of corruption into the glorious freedom of God's children. For we know that the whole creation has been groaning together with labor pains until now.

James 3:7-8

People can tame all kinds of animals birds, reptiles, and fish, but no one can tame the tongue.

I don't take this passage to mean that we should necessarily try to tame all kinds of animals, especially the wildlife. Yet reading this gives me some confidence in working with the wild ones until they are fully rehabbed and ready for release. Taming my tongue is a whole different topic...

Revelation 4:6-8

In front of the throne was a shiny sea of glass, sparkling like crystal. In the center and around the throne were four living beings, each covered with eyes, front and back. The first of these living beings was like a lion; the second was like an ox; the third had a human face; and the fourth was like an eagle in flight. Each of these living beings had six wings, and their wings were covered all over with eyes, inside and out. Day after day and night after night they keep on saying, "Holy, holy, holy is the Lord God, the Almighty—the one who always was, who is, and who is still to come."

Animals seem to be a fixture even in the heavenlies. We are told that God's throne is surrounded by creatures with features that are familiar to us from the animals we see here on earth. If God likes animals enough to feature them throughout the Bible, and even to have some form of them in

His heavenly Throne Room, surely, I tell myself, that's a legitimate reason for me to be crazy about them.

Revelation 5:5

Look, the Lion of the tribe of Judah, the heir to David's throne, has won the victory.

Our Savior certainly is the wild and victorious Lion of Judah in my mind and heart, along with being the sacrificial Lamb of God.

Revelation 5:13

I heard every creature in heaven and on earth and under the earth and in the sea. They sang: "Blessing and honor and glory and power belong to the one sitting on the throne and to the Lamb forever and ever."

Along with Psalms 148 and 150, this Revelation passage intimates that at some level, all creatures are capable of praising the Lord who made them.

Revelation 19:11-16 NKJV

Now I saw heaven opened, and behold, a white horse. And He who sat on him was called Faithful and True, and in righteousness He judges and makes war. His eyes were like a flame of fire, and on His head were many crowns. He had a name written that no one knew except Himself. He was clothed with a robe dipped in blood, and His name is called The Word of God. And the armies in heaven, clothed in fine linen, white and clean, followed Him on white horses. Now out of His mouth goes a sharp sword, that with it He should strike the nations. And He Himself will rule them with a rod of iron. He Himself treads the winepress of the fierceness and wrath of Almighty God. And He has on His robe and on His thigh a name written:

KING OF KINGS AND
LORD OF LORDS.

Jesus will come charging back to earth on a white horse, followed by His saints, also on horses. It therefore seems a reasonable assumption that there are some animals in heaven—horses at the very least. But never mind the horses! In the grandeur of this passage, we can only have eyes for the King. To the King of kings and Lord of lords I give all the glory, and I'll end these pages with this image from Revelation 19 of Him coming again.

Thank you for sharing my wildlife adventures with me, and may you and I also share someday in the wonders of God's kingdom yet to come—including new and unforeseen animal adventures for us all.

My Own Rescue Attempts:

WHAT WENT RIGHT, WHAT WENT WRONG

ACKNOWLEDGMENTS

First and foremost, I thank God for His inspiration and oversight, and for His intricate creation of all things furred and feathered. (And human, come to think of it.)

Next, I'm grateful to my husband, Michael, in whose path God constantly puts small creatures in need of help. Despite all my husband's characterizations of me as the animal nut, he is the one who keeps bringing them home, and everybody knows it. I have yet to see him pass by a turtle on the road without stopping to act as its crossing guard.

I'm also grateful to my three children, Patrick, Constance, and Dawn, and to their spouses, Jonna, Ronnie, and Matt, respectively. Although the numerous grandkids you have given (and will give) me don't have fur or feathers, they will certainly do. Collectively, you have all been more than obliging about sharing a portion of your mother's/grandmother's nurturing and love with the many little furred and feathered ones that have come along. Bless your huge hearts.

Thank you to my friend Jane Campbell, editorial director of Chosen Books, my constant mentor in all things editorial, and my constantly interested listener to all stories animal. You kept telling me to write this book, and any time I have taken your advice in the past, I have been grateful in the end. True again.

Thank you to acquisitions editor extraordinaire Kathleen Kerr and the entire team of Harvest House Publishers for coming alongside me in this book-publishing adventure. Besides wildly encouraging me by enjoying my wild stories, you took on the practical details of getting these pages into print. I'm pretty sure you did the lion's share of the work, while all I did was sit down and write.

Thank you to book agent Janet Kobobel Grant, president and

founder of Books & Such Literary Management. When I started this project, I had no idea how helpful having a book agent would be. Now, I have no idea how I could have done it without you.

Thank you to Brenda Sharp and my other wildlife rehabilitation mentors and friends, all of whom are willing to come alongside me with help, advice, and animal care as needed. Without the community of critter caregivers that you provide, it would be a lonely life—if there were ever any time to think about it. Which there isn't, ever. As you know.

Finally, I'm grateful to Skeeter, aka CoonieBear, the ring-tailed raccoon troublemaker who was my first, my favorite, and my friend. As far as I know, he is still nearby, living on the wild side in the woods out back. And that is just as it should be.

ABOUT THE AUTHOR

Trish Ann Konieczny is a licensed wildlife rehabilitator living in breathtaking Northern Michigan with her husband, Michael. By day Trish is a freelance editor, with 25 years of experience editing and ghostwriting Christian books for a national publisher. She calls herself a lover of God, family, and furry things, in that order (most of the time). Her work from home allows her to take frequent breaks to attend to any animals in her care, or to enjoy time with her three children, their spouses, and more than half a dozen grandchildren (whom she finds delightful, even though they have neither fur nor feathers).

You can contact Trish or find out more about her wildlife rehabilitation activities by visiting her online:

www.trishann.com

BIBLE TRANSLATIONS USED